Selkie Noticia
© Selkie Noticia
Self-published in the United States, 2021
Printed and Distributed by IngramSpark
Compiled and edited by Noëlle Cunningham, Rachel Firak, and Elizabeth Gross
Images provided by the British Library
ISBN: 9781735965406 (paperback)
ISBN: 9781735965413 (e-book)

SELKIE NOTICIA

AN ANTHOLOGY *of* VOICES BREAKING SILENCE

Compiled and edited by
Noëlle Cunningham, Rachel Firak, and Elizabeth Gross

A 'Selkie'

is a shape-shifting creature found in the folklore of the British Isles. The Selkie may slip out of its seal-like skin and appear as human on land, but grows weak as time passes away from the sea. Selkie tales often involve the loss or theft of a female Selkie's skin, which initiates a journey of regaining it. In some tales, a Selkie who has lost her skin sings to her sisters, who then bring her a new skin. In other versions, a Selkie's child—her creation—finds and returns her skin. The Selkie always finds a way to return to the sea, where it can once again be whole.

A 'Noticia'

after James Hillman's *notitia: an attentive noticing of the soul,* is a deeply human experience of listening both inward and outward as we forge our own unique imprint on this Earth, guided by the stories of survival and perseverance by others.

INTRODUCTION

You are holding in your hands a testament to the resilience of the human spirit.

Selkie Noticia is a nonfiction anthology on the theme of breaking silence. Our authors are people of diverse backgrounds, experiences and identities, each of us carrying a story that we once kept silent, but now feel ready to share.

Authentic stories are precious gifts in a world where there is so much praise for conformity, distraction, and disconnection from ourselves and each other. Yet true stories are not always easy to share, as they can contain difficult content from the teller's life. Accordingly, this book contains topics that may be considered taboo or otherwise sensitive. We invite the reader to approach this book with empathy and an open mind.

The courageous and vulnerable shares from our contributing authors have created a window through which the complexity of the human experience can be seen, both joyful and painful. It is our belief that by deeply listening to each other as we tell the tale, we create a container in which healing can occur.

The spark that ignites inside from a genuine thought shared or feeling expressed is no small magic— it lights the way to growth, wisdom, healing... to home.

Elizabeth, Rachel, and Noëlle

TABLE OF CONTENTS

MY NAME IS LEE YOKE LEE

Lee Yoke Lee

My name is Lee Yoke Lee.

At least that is how I have been named, called, and identified for nearly three decades of my life in Malaysia.

Then I came to America to start a family with the love of my life. I was called Yoke Lee Lee. The beautiful rhythm of my name is lost in this new system where you identify by first name and then last name.

At first, I accepted this passively. But over time it annoyed me. I mean, how hard is it to call someone by their preferred name, especially when that name is just one syllable? I get:

Yoke?

Yokee?

Yoko?

Even after I have indicated that they can call me Lee.

Finally, in 2019, I decided to stop being passive. I now politely but firmly tell people to call me Lee Yoke Lee, or Lee.

I still get the occasional Yoke, but I am not annoyed. It's likely they are thinking, "We are on a first-name basis," and mean no malice. I give them the benefit of the doubt.

Of course, there were a few thoughtful individuals who took the time and care to learn my name and to pronounce it properly.

To those who listened and paid attention, thank you for calling me by my preferred name. I feel seen and heard by you.

BUBBLES & BLADES

Theophania Madrason
(Tiffany Amber Madison)

She blows dollar store bubbles on the sidewalk. They smell like strawberries. Her hands are clean, but stained red from hair dye, or fake blood, she can't remember at this point. She thinks about the bag of stale weed under her bed, next to a love letter to a boy who broke her heart. The boy who promised he'd love her forever.

She has an infected spider bite on her upper thigh and her shoes smell faintly like cat piss. Her spine is slightly crooked, her teeth are pointed like fangs, and she has a 9-inch-long Y-shaped scar on her arm. People assume it's from a suicide attempt, but it's from slamming into a glass door when she was five.

These days, coupled with the scars from her genuine self-inflicted wounds, she can see why they might ask. But people have been asking since before she knew what suicide was. On occasion, she has theatrically told people she was attacked by a tiger at the circus. She even has a picture of her feeding a tiger with a bottle to add some substance to the tale. Sometimes people believe her. Other times they satisfy their gossip hard-on with an uncreative and hastily developed suicide attempt theory. But if she were going to kill herself, it wouldn't be with a blade. No, she thought to herself with finite aggravation, it would most definitely be with a leap of faith, or rather a lack thereof.

A cackling, angry cough floats out of the open window of her father's room. She sends a curtain of bubbles up around her and watches as they float through town, catching on mailboxes and traffic lights. She puts a wish into each one. A wish to leave this awful place. A wish for someone to steal her away. A wish for her mother to be well. A wish for her father to be kind, or at least shut the fuck up for an hour.

Wishes don't get you far in this town. It's the kind of place where you get knocked up or locked up by the time you're 25. She's 23, but she's already in a cage, just not the kind that comes with a jumpsuit. It's the kind with mint green walls and boxes piled high to the ceiling. The

neighbors can hear every manic episode she has, and the large curtainless
kitchen window provides a center-stage view of her morning mental
breakdowns to anyone walking the street. Her mother is dying, and the
doors all open backward. Her father, the Skeleton King, rules with an
iron fist and sings a narcissistic anthem at the break of dawn.

She has never been the girl next door, but she is the girl whose father
sleeps with a pistol in his sock, and she has had that pistol pointed at
her. He can never remember when she's said she's going out or coming
back, but he certainly keeps count of all his bullets.

The sidewalks here are spit-stained and smell perpetually of dog urine.
A car drives through town every morning at 3 am playing the Dukes of
Hazzard horn. Down the street, teenagers take shots of Jäger and play
rap on their porch. She wouldn't mind if they didn't throw their fucking
empty slushy cups into the street. They scream at her, but she just blows
another cloud of bubbles in response.

She can hear her neighbors talking about the bubbles and asking how
they got into their house. She chuckles to herself. She doesn't know
either. But she knows they might be magic.

A small boy and his father walk on the burning, salt-stained sidewalk.
The boy smiles at her and waves, but his father scowls. She's not sure if
it's her fishnets, black lipstick, or her low-cut top, but at this point, she
doesn't care. She gets dirty looks whether she dresses like a circus reject
or a 1940s French housewife. The boy and his father pass.

A cloud of bubbles floats into the road and a man in a truck slams on
his brakes. He honks his horn and flips her off, screaming something
about getting a job. She drops the bubble wand in surprise. What a
lovely Sunday afternoon. *Some people are just fucking miserable pricks no
matter what,* she thinks as she returns the sign with a fanged grin. The
man speeds off, and she is left with slippery hands and a cigarette butt
rolling towards her feet.

The bubbles pop in the branches above her. Somewhere inside the
house, the dog begins howling. A ribbon of curse words flows out
of the open window. Her mother, wearing a shabby purple bathrobe,

opens the door gingerly and pokes her head out. "Just wanted to make sure you were safe, sweetie," she coos. "Yeah ma, I'm okay," she says in a flat, gray tone. Her mother cringes as her father shouts from the bedroom. "I think your father wants something." Her mother's voice is apologetic and meek. The girl picks up the wand, wipes it in the grass, and blows another gust of bubbles. "Sure ma, I'll be there in a bit." Her mother's eyes are thankful but sunken. She shuffles back inside but leaves the door slightly ajar.

Across the street, a police car pulls up and parks. Its windows are down, and she can hear the officer protesting into his radio. "This is ridiculous man, it's just fuckin' bubbles, what the hell do you want me to do?" The officer rubs his eyes and throws his head back. He leans out of the window of the cruiser. "Hey kid, just, ah, try to keep the bubbles out of the road, okay?" The girl caps the bubbles, but not before blowing one more round. "Yeah, sure." Before he can say anything else, the girl stands up and walks toward the house.

The roof is crooked. She's certain there are mouse skeletons in the attic because she can hear them rolling around at night. The Skeleton King is coughing again. Everyone is sick. Everyone has always been sick. She is sick too, just not in the way you can see—unless, of course, she pulls back her sleeves to show you the pink and white lines that are scattered over her left arm.

The sweltering July heat has made the shoebox of a house nearly unbearable unless the AC is on. Her mother sleeps on the couch, and the dog neurotically chews his ass on the carpet. The cat is probably pissing somewhere new for her to find. She prays it isn't her room. There are no photos on the walls. It depresses her mother to see images of things that no longer are.

Stacks of dusty boxes and mountains of cat claw-torn bags reach the ceiling. Beyond them is a white door that doesn't quite shut right. On a sunny day, light trickles out through the cracks. This door leads to another world. Inside are talking dragons and goblin queens, wolf-girls, and lovesick demons. They all live, of course, within the pages of the girl's notebooks.

Her father, the Skeleton King, rattles out curses and demands. They assault her ears with vicious force. The girl clambers over the piles and makes her way to the stagnant chambers. There he sits, waist deep in ammo and anxiety. A yellowed air hose snakes itself from under the door to her father's nose. The air machine grumbles, a sound she has known well since childhood. Its rumbling, ancient motor whirrs a canticle of freshly filtered air. She checks to make sure it's on at highest capacity.

His tired, angry lungs press out a demand. "Pick the stuff up off the floor!" She stares. "This is what was so urgent?" Her voice is strong but cautious in its response. "Do it now, goddammit." And she does, like always.

Rubbing alcohol-soaked paper towels litter the floor on both sides of the hospital bed. "The trash is right there," she states. She points. It is a total of one foot away. She is aware that his lungs are tired. But if he can scream at her, he can save his breath. Another ribbon of gurgled curses flies from his mouth, belligerent and spiteful. *I could wrap those tubes around his throat,* she thinks. But she never does. The yellow snakes will keep him alive for now, she decides.

The air of the room is heavy and hot. When she cleans, he claims it stirs up the dust and chokes him. It's dark. The blinds haven't been opened in nearly two years. "It makes it easier for people to scope you out to fuckin' rob you!" he hisses.

He's not entirely wrong, she thinks, but she can't imagine anyone wanting to steal anything in this hoarder's palace of dead skin cells and repurposed laundry detergent piss jugs. Piss jugs. A small portion of her youth was spent explaining to her friends why she had to empty these mysterious jugs her father kept in the car and in the living room under his chair. A few lucky contenders have witnessed her father draping a green-and-white afghan over his lap to fill one up, perhaps while she was attempting to have some sad excuse for a tea party at her mother's ancient oak table, a family heirloom. The things that table has been privy to.

"Empty my piss jug," he snaps, half breathless but still angry enough to growl like a carriage driver from a Centurion novel. She is certain she's heard her father say that phrase more times than she's heard him say "I love you."

And everyone wonders why she is so depressed, she thinks. You grow up a little crooked when you're around death constantly, and you grow up neurotic with a father focused on civilization's impending doom. Her only goddamn solace in the world is within the confines of a notebook, but it's a notebook she has to keep secret. Because God forbid she speaks the truth about who and what she is, and what the fuck goes on inside this house. God forbid she writes about narcissistic fathers, suffocating saccharine mothers, and perverted uncles. Only happy things. Sad, unpleasant things are not allowed.

Sadness is disrespectful. She has to be cheerful the moment she pries her aching body out of bed and slinks into the family room. "There's nothing for you to be depressed about!" her mother insists. "Why the fuck can't you stop being a miserable bitch?" her father seethes.

She hates to disappoint. Which is precisely why she doesn't dare see a therapist, because it's a taboo fuckin' subject. Even if she had the insurance, seeing a therapist would be a cataclysmic event. Her father forbids such an affair, because somehow drawing attention to her illness will alert "THEM." "THEY" will have the police talk to her father. And "THEY" will take her father's guns away. She's starting to wish whoever "THEY" are would take her the fuck away, too. Someone, just fucking someone take her away, because she doesn't have the heart or courage to leave this hell house.

Maybe that's why she fantasizes about being abducted. Anything is better than losing her damn sanity in a place that's supposed to help her become a fully functional human, but instead has made her anxious and paranoid, and very depressed. She's afraid to leave. And while it's on her to make the choice, there are a hell of a lot of reasons she chooses to stay.

Reruns of CSI and Law and Order Special Victims Unit continually blare from the living room. For the last 20 years, she's been fed subliminal messages from a 24-inch screen that everyone is going to rape her, murder her, and stuff her into a drain pipe. Dinner is eaten with body bags and sirens on the television. Breakfast is eggs with a side of two bodies found in a car trunk. For lunch, she watches a POV recording of a girl being assaulted.

These images are supplemented with her father's anecdotal stories of his glory days as a P.I. and "bounty hunter." And while she's certain the stories have some truth to them, she also can't help but wonder how exaggerated they have become over the years. Day after day, she consumes these victims' stories. Mother just doesn't have the energy to argue about changing the channel anymore. Cancer tends to murder the spirit, not just the body.

There are mountains of dirty bedsheets on her mother's antique chair in the bathroom. The old wooden legs are gouged from cat claws and weak from being dragged across the linoleum floor. The chair was a symbol of everything her mother tried so hard to build, now cast to the side and engulfed with the same sickness the rest of the house had contracted. It wasn't a matter of having time to wash them, but of how many times her father could soil them in a 24-hour period, on account of his prideful rejection of adult diapers.

She completes her task and returns the jug. Her escape is smooth, as her father is preoccupied with counting the empty Abreva cartridges and rusty disposable razors he keeps for the impending apocalypse. You never know what you may be able to trade or reuse. Because in the apocalypse, she muses, there is a high market for germ-infested medical items. She climbs through the door and back into the living room, over the creeping bags of old air hoses and water-filled Ensure bottles, into the solace of her bedroom.

This is a healing place, in the Mad House. She has covered the hospital-green walls with a thousand things to distract from the ungodly hue. Lace and harlequin masks, hanging bells and feathers, torn pages from the carcasses of salvaged antique novels, strands of dripping pearls. A stoic army of porcelain dolls forms a barricade around her shelves and headboard. Their eyes threaten mutiny and tea-tossing disobedience.

The scent of lilacs and roses greets her as she hastily burrows under her red throw blanket. Every object has been carefully chosen to make this room into a sanctuary, down to the blue fairy lights that hang above the window. At night they bathe her in azure elegance. She brings the glowing cosmos down into the Skeleton King's dark, dusty castle. She grows a garden of hope in a place that suffocates her name.

Her prized collection of books rests in the headboard shelves. These are the guardians of her dreamland. In between the perfectly lined spines of these books, a small slip of paper peeks out. Her fingers reach out to touch it, a prayer-like ritual that she has come to practice. One day, soon, this slip of paper will be her ticket to leave. But she must open the door. And she has to leave behind the angry Skeleton King, and her dying mother. It would be so much easier, she thinks, if someone took her away.

She looks at her hands. They are clean, but stained red. She is guilty, guilty of being afraid.

HERE

Katrina Washington

Death has never unsettled me. No matter how sudden or unnecessary, it has never shaken me. I find this to be an odd revelation; a random fact about myself I must come to terms with as it continuously proves to be true. As cliché as it sounds, I am another black girl from the ghetto—yet never critically tainted by the fruits of ghetto trees. I peacefully co-exist in this world I was born into. Besides the sharp annoyance we feel when someone argues Chicago not having an east side, I am nothing like my peers. (And for the record, we do have an east side. Take the time to drive to Paxton Avenue, anywhere from 67th to 71st street, and you will find yourself not only in my neighborhood, but on the east side of Chicago.) Here is home, a common ground we all started in and we all return to. Although we've chosen different paths, the fact remains that we're friends. I've tearfully observed four of them being lowered into their resting places. One of them died too close, and all too soon. Even more have found themselves caught in their own twisted webs of crimes, and ultimately trapped in a caged hell. Jail is home here, too. On Paxton, the steady flow of disappearances, to whichever hell, have always hurt but have never shocked me.

You see the struggles of my community on the faces of all its inhabitants. Our children's faces are painted with confusion, not sure where they belong or who they belong to. Gangs have convinced them that they can find the family they lack in the unity of a loose-fitting brotherhood. Our elders show a removed acceptance for the way things are. It is hard to teach those who do not want to be taught. They have decided to save their wasted words for those who choose to listen. In a time when no one listens. The addicted have no faces at all. Only a need for what kills them. The faces of thugs, dealers, and the women and men who glorify them suggest triumph. In their own twisted reality, they have the block on lock. Within the rubble of a torn community, they find their own version of solitude. And then there are people like me. I'm not sure what my face reads. It probably shows longing. Anger. I wish I could make them more like me. More removed. But no one wants to leave. They have accepted their place here. In hell.

August 31, 2009 upheld the Paxton legacy. I remember the beautiful weather. The sun glistened on rain puddles from the previous day's thunderstorm. The clouds looked like cotton candy, pearly white, and thick enough to carry an entire family across the world. Or at least out of here. A picture would have looked like a postcard. The summer of 2009 forgot to bring her blistering heat, so this was an abnormally good day. Even the black and white rats with wings that hang in the empty lot next to the dollar store seemed to be in cheerful moods as they shared the discarded contents of a Harold's Chicken lunch special. The coos of the pigeons were drowned out by the ice cream truck, which announced its presence with that one familiar song that I can never sing. Even now, the lyrics still lie permanently stuck on the tip of my tongue. I remember thinking, "what a beautiful sight," as brown children in pastel colors ran safely beside it. I blamed my feeling that something was wrong on my natural desire to sabotage anything good.

It bothers me that beautiful days in the hood are so few and far between, that when they occur you have no choice but to savor them. Question them, even. The week before, someone held up the Currency Exchange and killed an elderly woman on his escape route. A kid was hit by a car while running from the police two days ago and died yesterday. There is probably over $15,000 worth of drugs sold on my block alone, daily.

I didn't dwell on the feeling for long, because a familiar neighborhood face was approaching. He was short and fat and to the untrained eye, probably the toughest guy in the bunch. But a closer look revealed chestnut brown eyes that could find beauty in everyone, a crooked smile with childlike mischief, and hands that could cover and keep yours warm while you waited for the morning bus. On Paxton, a man is nothing without his nickname. His was Twist. To me, he's affectionately "Twister," or "Tasty," when I feel like embarrassing him in front of everyone else. I enjoy it because the sexual context always raises an eyebrow or two. It's actually a harmless little inside joke that will remain as such forever, I assume.

"Bina (a girl is nothing without a nickname either, apparently), let's go to Target and get a baseball and bat. We're going to play with the kids today."

This was typical Twist; thoughtful, random, and playful. It's funny. I've known him for about ten years but have never heard of or seen him with any family. Some things you just don't talk about. These are the codes of the street. As he put his arm around my shoulder and joked about demolishing me in baseball, I realized I didn't mind playing family with him and didn't need to know anything more than that.

"Let's go around the corner. Yola is in the car, he's going to ride too," said Twist.

If Paxton had an American Gangster, Yola would have been it. Yola was a strong, tall, butterscotch man with a smile as bright as the August sun that day. I met Yola during a difficult time. I was ten, and had just celebrated my friend Tre's birthday with him and some other kids at Odyssey Fun World three months before. My male best friend, who was killed last year, was explaining to me that he and Tre could no longer hang together because "Tre lives on Chappel and that's the wrong side of Clyde. He with them other niggas now." Yola explained to us that cutting ties with people in certain parts of the area would be safer for everyone. He seemed to mean what he said while being angry while he said it. I always wondered why Yola chose a life on the streets. He had a mind much larger than he gave it credit for. It was full of knowledge that he wasn't quite sure what to do with.

Our second encounter set the tone for all the others.

"History does nothing. It does not possess immense riches, it does not fight battles. It is men, real, living, who do all this. Women too, Katrina. Remember that," said Yola.

Your average street thug probably doesn't go around quoting Marx when the neighborhood girls fail a history test. But this is what Yola had to say when I came home hating history. His advice was funny like that. It wasn't always right or appropriate, but it sure did sound good. As I opened the door to Yola's black 2009 Infiniti truck, I was bombarded by the sultry voice of Nina Simone trying to make us understand that you can have nothing but still have life. Not your average street thug.

Today was going to be a good day. After arguing with Twist all the way to the store and back about playing girls against boys, I finally got my way. Everyone was ready but me. I was stalling because I had called in the reinforcements. I was in the process of changing into a dingy t-shirt and some cut-offs when my neighbor Ashley called. She and the girls were ready. I was happy everyone was in the mood to play because we had shit to prove. Twist didn't think girls were good baseball players. I bet him $20 that there was no disadvantage for women if we played girls against boys.

Thirty seconds after hanging up, I heard thunder. But not from Mother Nature. Shots fired. You can never tell exactly where they are coming from but I knew these were close. I remember thinking, "Gunshots this early in the day?" I called Twist's phone, but there was no answer. Gangbangers don't always schedule gun activity, but every now and then they let us girls know when the block is going to be hot so we can stay off it. No warning today, so it must have been enemy fire.

Not yet panicked, I waited a couple of seconds and went outside when Twist didn't call back. Ambulances and fire trucks were hurrying to the south side of 71st street. Someone was hit. In the hood, sirens play a familiar song. Red, white, and blue lights were flashing like the fourth of July. But it was no holiday. As I reach the commotion, my knees buckle and lose focus on walking.

A black 2009 Infiniti truck is bashed into the light pole. The front windshield has shattered and the driver's door is open. I see two large shoes touching the pavement as if Yola is sitting up, about to get out of the car. But he isn't. As I slowly approach, I see that he is dead. Twist is lying on the sidewalk and paramedics are screaming words I cannot understand. Not because it's medical jargon but simply because I just can't understand. By now, the crowds have formed. Kids are looking at their destiny. People are screaming out.

"Is Yola okay?"
"Who did it?"
"Aye man, who was in the car with him? Who that on the ground?"
"Is that Twist? That nigga breathing?"
I finally hear a police officer say, "Ma'am, you have to move to the other side of the tape."

They've taped up another crime scene on Paxton. I can tell by the officer's tone that this is not the first time he has told me to move. So I move. I take my place on the north side of the street with the other spectators, separated from the scene by train tracks. Everyone wants to know if Yola is still breathing because they can't exactly see from where they are standing. I know the answer but I don't want to say, because in that moment, it would have made it too real.

If the only murder scene you've ever seen was on television, you'd never know that they don't move bodies for a while. After Twist is rushed to the hospital and Yola remains where he is, common sense and the fact that we've all seen this before answers the question. Yola is dead.

The streets cry out for their Frank Lucas. Their Bumpy Johnson. Gang members stand guard but are unable to hide the fact that even thugs cry. Channel 5, 7, and 9 are here. Police are walking through the crowds talking to people who learned as children to stay silent around the police.

It angers me that for once the neighborhood came together. In death. We were all there. Not at the neighborhood watch meeting, but at the crime scene. I see the owners of the corner store, the beauty supply, and Harold's Chicken workers. The alderman. My neighbors are standing here. My friends are crying here. We're not at PTA meetings discussing education and curriculum. We are here. Too late to save another life.

It didn't cross my mind until days later, at the funeral, when the preacher mentioned Yola's last moments, that I was in that car twenty minutes prior. It was and still is a constant inner battle of mine. These are my friends. But I'm scared to death that they will kill me. Not intentionally or directly, but dead is dead. This is my life. Can't even play a fucking game of baseball with friends. As the pastor recalled funny moments from his time with Yola, I thought about that baseball game we will never play. Or how things might have been different if we hadn't lost the baseball equipment the last time we played. We might have already been in the field playing.

What-ifs rarely work well in these situations. I'm hurt, but not surprised. This is what we do here. Die.

My mother used to always say her goal in life was to give the preacher something more to talk about than the Bible. "A preacher that don't do nothing but quote the Bible must not have much to say about the person laying in that casket. Hell, we can talk about the Bible on Sunday," she'd say after every funeral.

I thought about my mother's words on the day of Yola's funeral. Not only was the line to view the body around the corner, but the family announced that after the reading of the obituary, the Lord's Prayer, and a song, the remaining time would be spent hearing from family and loved ones who wanted to speak because so many people expressed a desire to share a memory. I wished my mom was there to see all that my friend had accomplished. But she stopped coming to neighborhood funerals years ago. When I got home and handed over her requested obituary, she placed it in a shoebox with the others and hopes and prays she doesn't have to reopen that shoebox anytime soon. She will.

As I brought my attention back to how crowded the church was, I realized what was happening was a beautiful thing in itself. Death does not always bring folks together. There are such things as empty funerals, and obituaries with no memories. These senseless killings create rifts between age groups, and form animosity between each other, the police, the wrong, and the right. Tragedy does not always bring a community together. Yola's tragedy did. Not your typical street thug.

I stole a glance at Twist. What should feel like a blessing and another chance at life is instead a burden. He is angry at himself sitting with a bullet in his arm, while Yola's the one in the casket. I cannot imagine wanting to die, or sitting in a funeral wishing there was another casket for me there. But this is what he feels. He told me so as we drove to the burial together. It is customary, or at least as far as I know, to drive through the deceased's neighborhood en route to the burial site. It almost seemed inappropriate because there was no way to avoid the corner he died on. Did we want to remember that today? But I imagine Yola wouldn't have wanted it any other way. He was one of the ones with the look of triumph on his face. He, ironically, loved the neighborhood that killed him.

I finally convinced Twist to take a look at the obituary. It was beautiful and full of memories; scrapbook-like. I glanced in the rearview mirror, where Twist was sitting and caught him smiling for the first time in days. He was reading the part I hoped he would: "Yola leaves behind many cherished friends. First and foremost, Twist. The one God chose to be there with Yola as He prepared him for rebirth."

We left the funeral and went home and played a game of baseball. Sort of like our own repast to Yola. Girls against boys, in honor of the last time Yola decided on teams for the block. Yola was on my side with that one. He knew girls could play just as good, if not better, than the boys. We won. Of course, Twist claims the win was hugely related to the fact that his bum arm kept him on the sidelines. On Paxton, we mean what we say about money. Small or large amounts, silly or serious reasons, a bet is still a bet. I took that $20 and bought Yola's favorite drink, Hennessey. I joked with myself and thought, typical street thug.

Later that evening, I joined the rest of the neighborhood close to the crime scene. We gathered once more in front of Yola's shrine. I had never seen one so huge. There were so many balloons, teddy bears, cards, and posters with enough signatures to get someone elected into office. But we'd never use our power like that. I pull out the Hennessey, take a swig, and pour out the rest for Yola. I say a silent prayer in hope that we will remember how easily we can gather together. Maybe even for a different cause.

The police drive by and say they'll leave us alone if we don't make too much noise and promise to have the block cleared in a couple of hours. We're in a peaceful mood, so we pretend we all have curfews and agree. Days later, the police superintendent will order the police to tear the shrine down due to it being unlawful to post things on city property without the city's permission. They will tear it down in front of us without offering the chance to do it ourselves and keep the memories. I'll help move the shrine to a different location while cursing out every police officer in the vicinity. All hell will break loose before Channel 2 arrives on the scene for interviews.

"What the the fuck you doing, pig?"
"Don't touch our shit, muthafucka."
"You wanna go to jail or go home? You're mad? Take it up with my boss

and kiss my ass in the process!"
"Lock up anybody who gets any closer."

It is in that moment, I will realize that maybe I have more in common
with these people than what you see on the surface. Anger and presence,
among other things. But for now, as I empty the last of Yola's Hennessey,
we are here. Peaceful.

OPEN WINDOW

Anonymous

Frankie was one of those "what the hell was I doing" guys. I was ten years his junior on a strong career path, full of ambition and way too serious for my own good. He was in his 40's, divorced father of two with a wicked sense of humor and way too into his record collection. I had been trying to shake my habit of dating bad boys, but every now and then a girl just wants to have fun. Plus, he worked in the restaurant industry, and there's something a little extra going on with that crowd. The heat of the kitchen, front of house/back of house drama, obscene customers, the self-medication of booze and drugs—all these ingredients make up a whole personality type that's usually pretty spicy.

Frankie would get off work waiting tables at an upscale steakhouse around 1:00am (already way past my bedtime). I would Uber over to his place with a bottle of booze in my overnight bag, and we would do a bunch of coke and dance around in the kitchen. I would listen to him ramble on about punk rock or disco as he cooked me elaborate, delicious dinners—which always seemed like a miracle to me because he only ever had White Claws and condiments in his fridge. He taught me how to make a perfect steak on a cast iron. Some nights we would stay up for hours just chatting and watching shows, and not have sex at all. That's when I learned what coke dick was (look it up).

When we did have sex, Frankie liked it dirty. He was a wild guy in bed. We had many playful, outrageous nights together, and more than anything he loved anal sex. I hadn't played around with it that much so I enjoyed experimenting. Still not my favorite thing, but hey, variety is the spice of life. I became familiar with the after-effects, and made sure to spend a little extra time in the bathroom afterwards, straightening out my insides.

One night, that fateful night that will live in infamy, Frankie was over at my place. We had just finished a rousing session of butt sex, and I crawled off the bed and stood up. As I was rearranging myself, I could feel all the air that was pumped in and out of my ass had created some giant bubbles, and they were working their way back out. Way too fast. Too fast!! Resistance was futile—unable to barricade against the blast, a tornado blasted through my butthole—"WRRAAAAAPPHHHHH." My face, frozen in horror, masked secret relief that I had not, in fact, shat on the floor. It was a bold, terrific, well-rounded event. We both let out a laugh—it wasn't like it was the first time we'd farted in front of each other. But the laugh quickly turned into screams.

"Oh my God what the fuck?!?" "OPEN THE WINDOW! OPEN THE GODDAMN WINDOW!!"

The fumes assault our senses and our eyes start to water as both of us begin to wail—a slow, building wail as our brains register the intense, unrelenting gas bomb I just dropped. Frankie was into raunchy shit, but I took it way too far. I had just expelled the most rancid, putrid fart of my entire lifetime. Worse than rotting garbage. Worse than dog shit. Imagine the most disgusting thing you've ever smelled. Doesn't even come close. I'm sputtering and coughing as I scramble for relief—lighting incense, turning on the fan, waving air out the open window with sheets of paper. Frankie dove underneath the covers, all the while screaming at me:

"*Goddamn woman!!!* What crawled up your butt and died?? Seriously?!?" "YOU!" I yell right back. "Your own goddamn sperm, you nasty man! You put it there!"

We keep screeching as if we're being pelted by acid rain. Frankie won't open up the covers even a peep for me to crawl back in my stinky shame. I'm mortified, but what can I do? I imagine our neighbors hearing all of this, screams bouncing off the brick walls in the alley and onto porches below. I honestly don't care if they hear, as long as that deadshitspermgarbagewater smell doesn't waft through an unsuspecting open window. Dogs would bark. Babies would wake up crying. Bouquets of flowers would shrivel and brown. Even the rats would run from that smell. Briefly, part of me wonders if there's something fundamentally wrong with my body, but no—this gas monster was definitely a team effort.

Eventually Frankie opened up the covers, our bellies heaving up and down, both of us exhausted from laughing/crying. He could have left, but he stayed. I couldn't leave, I was already home. Forced to live in my absurd, uncooperative body. My home of shifting organs and sounds and smells. My home of belly-laughs and painful tears. My home for life.

MEMORIES OF MOTHS, MOTHERS, AND CHILDREN

Xavier Vilar-Brasser

A moth landed on the screen of my open, late-winter window. A spindly-legged and silver-winged specter of the shadows settling into a tight almond shape, it sat speckled dark and grey against the heavy snow melting in the fluorescent glow of the alley below. I held an Irish coffee in one hand, and a cigarette burning through its filter in the other. The Rolling Stones' "Sister Morphine" throbbed the floorboards of my apartment, slide guitar sinking my body back against the wall, bathed in pulsing neon blues, pinpoint pupils strained to see the light.

"The scream of the ambulance is soundin' in my ear.
Tell me, sister morphine, how long have I been lying here?
What am I doing in this place? Why does the doctor have no face?"

This was last week, before I started trying to get clean, before my admission of addiction. It must have been near three in the morning—not especially late for me, my sleep cycle screwed by pendulous swings between mania and immobilizing depression. Before I met my moth—my momentary moonlit muse, my Moses—I sunk religiously into self-indulgent self-destruction, surrounded by searing solitude and my own silent swearing. Trying to live like Keith Richards, and living no life at all. I had spent months assuming the weight of guilt and failure over an illness beyond my control, bound and bludgeoned by bipolar disorder. Smothered by something immaterial, irrational, inescapable, and inherent, I found myself consumed by the drone of my own empty apologies. I swigged and smoked and snorted in seclusion, slipping away from myself—a sullen and desolate silhouette in quarantine.

For an instant, we were plural: two nocturnal beings, petulant pests of the night poised cold and alone, together but separated by a wire mesh stitched with the intention to *keep out*. My moth must have spent most of the winter seeking asylum from the Midwestern freeze inside our artificial shelter, where we find refuge from the humbling indifference of all that is natural. When shooed out into the cutting cold, when somewhere some drawer or door was pulled open to shock and screech, my moth learned of its role as a nuisance. It was unwanted, and found my island of exile, my home and vagrant haven—a place where the left and lost can lie.

I've always found it fascinating how much we villainize moths—a scourge to sterile silks and crops. The Old English origin of the word *moth*, derived from the root of *midge*, has a foul reputation rooted deeply and inseparably within its meaning: *"especially referring to a pest that devours fabrics."* Nuisance, by nature, is embedded in its name. But can we really be blamed for tarring them with this demonic epithet? After all, it's what they do. They come in, tearing land and home to shreds, invasive species devouring forests with a seemingly limitless appetite for carnage. It's easy to point a finger at something small enough to be squashed by one, and even easier to do so without acknowledging the stains of hypocrisy lingering in the dusty residue transferred to our skin from their wings.

Don't these damn moths know of our righteous supremacy? Those are *our* God-granted forests to demolish. God, in whose awkward image we were made, loosed us upon the world with a commandment to spread and invade.

The truth, contrary to the one we're told, is that these cloth-chomping cretins comprise only a handful of some 160,000 species of moths. Those with a taste for textiles are mostly confined to members of the Tineidae family—just one of the many families within the order Lepidoptera. Despite their reputation, an overwhelming majority of moth species (such as the Luna, Plyphemus, Atlas, Promethea, and Cecropia, just to name a notable few) don't even have mouths. They couldn't pose less of a threat to our autocracy. But that won't stop us from branding every moth with broad and baseless labels.

The Luna moth is among the most breathtaking organisms I've had the privilege of seeing. With bright, lime-green wings reaching up to 5 inches in diameter, these ethereal and delicate giants are more stunning than any butterfly species ever to grace a garden or tattoo. Even so, their ever-declining numbers are routinely slashed in waves by our pesticides in a type of nuclear devastation worthy of their neon-glowing appearance. We'll do anything, so long as it gets the job done, so long as it protects us and keeps us safe—and you'd have to be a fool to believe this credo distinguishes between elegance and nemesis.

My grandmother Lyn adored Luna moths with an appreciation that almost bordered on worship. I'm told that before the car crash, she wrote poems and made up fairy tales about them to tell my mother at bedtime. They all contained the core theme of the moth as a symbol of hope, for she saw them as angels long before she went to fly among them.

Lyn was killed by a drunk driver when my mother was roughly my age, somewhere between 20 and 23. I never had the privilege of meeting her, though I'm constantly told by my family members how much I bear her resemblance—an honor I have incessantly endeavored to live up to, and cried on the countless occasions I have failed to do so. She was unimaginably talented and intelligent, the matriarch of my messy family on my mother's side. A Mensa member, community organizer, awarded debater, and teacher, she even started her own theater company in Chicago. How could I ever do such greatness justice? I'll never understand why my family would utter such blasphemy to her memory by comparing us.

I've tried to write about Lyn many times, but ultimately abandoned each attempt, for fear that my relative lack of brilliance would disgrace the legacy of her existence. Seeing that moth clutch the screen the other day, though, instilled me with something, and inspired me just enough to try again. And I'll keep trying, trying to wrestle some meaning from the unjust cruelty of chance. Trying to honor the life of someone I never knew, but have always known to be a part of me.

After Lyn's death, my mother took to drugs and drinking, rapidly developing a severe dependence on vodka and Vicodin that would govern her until we had our own drunk-driving accident. I watched from the back seat as a telephone pole became as much a part of the car as its chassis, and my mother's forehead splintered the glass of the windshield, which stuck there in her flesh like a bloody, crystal crown. My family snapped to attention and into action. By the time I got out of the hospital, she had already been sent to rehab, and it would be six months before we were allowed to visit. That glass crown smeared with blood still stings my eyes like the dust from the airbag flirting with the fumes of the thick engine flames. The loneliness of that six months still gnaws somewhere deep inside my heart.

"We'll be okay, I promise," I said to the moth as it flew off. I lit another smoke as my feather-light companion fluttered out of sight and into the freeze. I was left with a familiar feeling of comfort and security being wrenched away from me, like a blindfold torn from my eyes too quickly, suddenly crashing into a world I'm not ready to see on my own. The wind whipped across my face and whispered promises of something more than drunken days and drug-numbed nights. In the wake of that moth's company, I lingered on the load of my seclusion, and my heart froze with a sense of longing for what could never return. I still haven't shaken that sensation: the pressing horror of my isolation and addiction, the inheritance of anguish.

When I was 12 years old, my mother was fresh out of rehab and it seemed like all the heat of hell was finally cooling. On the day I moved back in with her, she picked me up in a new car, jammed with suitcases of all my belongings. A bag of the letters she sent me from the facility in California was tucked between my knees. We were returning to the place we were both struggling to call home, returning to reclaim it from the stench of the memories of her downward spiral. We pulled into the driveway and she looked at me with a smile as she pressed a button on the keychain that opened the garage door.

It seemed like a small thing, but it meant a lot to me that we had that simple and unnecessary convenience. It meant no more running around to the side door in the cold rain so we could open the main door and pull the car in. It meant no more difficulties, no more pain—it meant that things would finally be getting better. It meant hope.

As the door creaked and rose, an explosion of hundreds of moths erupted from the long-unopened garage, flying through bicycle spokes and toolboxes into the fluorescent parking lot. It turned out that the garage had been infested while my mother was in rehab, and no one was around to keep things running smoothly.

I let out a childish scream, now that I again had the ability, comfort and security to indulge in such petty things, while tears slid down the cigarette wrinkles on my mother's cheeks. I thought she was overwhelmed by the bother, and I instantly panicked that it would be enough to trigger one of the relapses that I had spent countless hours researching and dreading. I hadn't yet learned much about my grandmother Lyn, so all I saw was a pest. But there was something different in those sobs—a confusing complex of grief and belief. As moths sailed around us in a daze of darting, whipping wings, I watched the mother I'd finally been given back cry for the mother she'd lost.

ADDENDUM TO 2.2.13 ACCIDENT

Rachel Firak

Two days after we return from the hospital, I have my first dream of you since your death.

I'm sitting in a restaurant we used to visit together. I'm alone, bruised and beaten up. I see your parents come in. They sit on the opposite side of the room. At first separate, we come together. I go for a walk with your brother and feel comforted by his presence.

When I come back to the restaurant, I see you talking to the hostess. You're trying to pay our bill, but you don't have any money. So I pay instead. When I see you, I run up and squeeze you. "I love Collin," I say. You hug me back.

You ask how we are doing. I tell you all of this has been extremely hard, but sometimes we feel you with us, and that helps us cope. You ask if we are all working together. I say we are, so much. You ask how I'm doing. I say that I'm going to be okay.

—

I move into your parents' house because I can't bear to be home.
The state trooper meets me there.
He's our age, or a little younger. His tone is gruff and authoritative.
From where I sit I can see your picture, your siblings' pictures, on the wall.
He shows me the names of everyone involved in the accident.
He says that no one can verify my version of the events.
He recites their combined memory: that I tried to pass when there wasn't enough space, that the person in front of us was neither going too slow initially nor sped up to prevent us from passing.
Their consensus that I was the one, solely, that made a mistake.
Responsible for your death.
And that they are sorry for my loss.

I feel like a child, surrounded by adults who KNOW.
They talk about us in hushed tones.
They did or didn't know you, did or didn't know me. But they saw us
around, or knew your parents.
Their relatives send cards to this address.
"The whole community mourns with you," the trooper says.
He drives away.

My parents want me to get a lawyer.
Your parents don't want me to.
I can't handle it anyway.
I plead guilty to "failure to keep right" and "unsafe passing."
Ulysses Town Court sends me a bill for $470.
I accumulate 18 points on my license.
The DMV fines me $400 for a "Driver Responsibility Assessment."
A trivial fee for losing you.

My insurance company needs pictures of the car.
I can't bear it, so your parents drive to Koskinen's to take them.
They rescue our things left inside, dented and stained with blood—
yours.
I knew there would be blood because I remember waking up to it, bright
and beautiful, as the firefighters cut the top off the car.
It was pooled and frozen in puddles in the floor of the front seats.

—

I dream I'm on the streets of Philly, chasing you. You're curly-haired
and carefree in the car ahead; I'm exasperated as I try to follow your
trail. We end up in a restaurant across the street from the accident. I
come in, sit down beside you. Wait for me, sit by me, lay by me, Collin—
is it too much to ask?

I dream you meet your end in a gladiator sport. Over time, you lose
your mental capacities, your physical strength. I witness every glancing
blow, every fire, knowing you are less you with each one. Your last days
in a hospital before you finally die—someone, a nurse, explains to me
that people always tell themselves their loved one was ready to go. The
truth is, no soul leaves willingly. It wasn't meant to happen. It never is.

Oh Collin, I'm so sorry.

—

My mom wants to bring me back to Ohio.
I say I want to stay with your family instead.
I spend every day with your parents. We eat together, talk, cry together.
They tell me they love me.
I tell them I love them.
They help me.
We help each other.

I go back to our cabin.
Seeing your shoes left so sweetly by the door gives me quite a reaction.
I torture myself with doubt.
I wouldn't be reckless, would I?
With the two most important people in my world in the car: you and me?
Our cat, fed by neighbors while we were gone, crawls into my lap as I sit by the fire, so trusting.
I think, she doesn't know what I've done.

When I crawl into bed that night, I say out loud:
"Goodnight, Collin. I love you."
The words ring through the empty cabin, bounce off the walls, drop to the floor and shatter. They elicit horror when they reach my ears.

—

I dream I'm the widow of a much older man. I'm not that sad. His relatives gather in the swimming pool outside. I hear your voice, telling a joke. "(Person's first name) (verb-ing) (person's last name)?—I won't," you say coyly. Everyone laughs hard, I laugh too. I wrap my towel around me and approach, still dripping. You're grinning from ear to ear. "That is probably the last best joke you'll ever tell," I say, and lean down to kiss you. Your lips taste like the hospital chemicals. I love you and feel proud to be your lover.

I dream I'm wandering through my high school, unable to go to class.

Someone offers to help me. "I might take you up on that," I say, knowing I never will. When I remember that you're dead, the equation of my life becomes unsolvable, doesn't make sense. I drag myself into crawl spaces, decide this is where I'll stay. I write your name on the walls. I carve it out of wood and fiberglass insulation.

—

My car insurance company sends me 139 pages of medical bills and denials of claim.

I read my diagnoses: "Subdural and Subarachnoid Hemorrhage Following Injury," "Closed Fracture: Base of Skull," "Closed Fracture: Malar and Maxillary Bones," "Intercranial Injury: Other and Unspecified," "Compression of Brain," "Concussion, With Loss of Consciousness."

I learn from the bills that I was delirious and vomited in the ambulance on the way to Guthrie in Sayre, PA.

I vaguely remember the wheelchair I used in the hospital.

I never receive detailed summaries of your medical care. Your parents do.

My medical bills total $83,331.24.

Yours total over $300,000.00.

My car insurance agrees to pay $11,086.20.

Their letters say that though they are denying most of the claims, they will work with the hospital "to spare you unnecessary involvement in disputes about bill payment."

The hospital never sends me anything, but the bills go away.

—

I'm in bed, upset, and you are there. I reach out my arms, requesting a hug. "I'm coming!" you say. You joke that since we're both here, in the same place at the same time, we can't help but collide. You lower yourself over me, falling with gravity into my arms. I wake on a deep inhale, breathing you in.

I dream I'm leading you to your newly rented bedroom. You're exhausted, having just come from a run. We walk through a narrow passageway to reach it. As I grasp the doorknob and turn, you wrap your arms around me from behind. Is the door stuck? Is the door locked? To your final resting place, we never make it—just us in the hallway, in love and loving again.

—

In a half-dream state, my subconscious asks: How did Collin die?
I rack my brains, siphon, and read the sediment at the bottom like tea leaves.
"He died in a car accident," I reply.
Then the unanswerable question:
What the hell does that mean?

My new doctor diagnoses me with "Adjustment Disorder with Depression" so I can claim temporary disability from work.
I have to see her regularly to extend it.
Each time we play a game: she asks me if I'm considering suicide, I tell her I don't have the will to carry it out, she says she's glad to hear it and signs my forms.

I get therapy.
My therapist encourages me to feel my feelings, not shut them off.
It is the most enormously difficult thing I've ever done.
I learn to tolerate the anguish, terror, and pain, and locate the feelings in my body.
I become stronger. The guilt resolves. My perception of the event changes. Less horror, more holy.
On a scrap of paper, I write, "from SCARED to SACRED"

I buy your car from your parents.
The first time I drive since the accident, it's just repositioning it in front of our cabin. Your dad suggests I do this to check its battery life.
I put the key in the ignition and turn. The wipers slide across the windshield. The last time you drove your car it was raining. Or was it snowing?
This seems important to note, like the contents of your wallet, or the last text message you ever sent me.
I wait to see how I react. I don't know what I'm expecting. Blacking out?

Uncontrollable crying?
Nothing happens.
I turn the car back off.

—

I dream Simone and Jaya have a child with eagle's wings. On a rocky mountaintop, I copy this child's movements in order to be healed. We bend together, we fold together, we chant. I know that I am deeply wounded. It will be a very long process.

In the worst dream yet, I realize I haven't heard from you in months. Did we break up? I try to call you. You must have changed your number in the breakup. Email address too. I search the internet for signs of your life. I want to find you. I want you to come back. I'm sure we could have worked it out. Why did we separate in the first place? I struggle to remember, instead recall a letter you once wrote that ends in "Thank you for everything" with a million tiny hearts. Collin. Breaking up is not possible in the universe in which you sent that letter. But death is. My body is jolted from sleep as I confront this truth for the thousandth time.

These few minutes I spend in bed, crying and asking you where you went—these are the hardest moments of my life.

—

Nobody wanted to, but finally someone—a child—asks:

"What does 'grief' mean?"

I attempt an answer.

"Grief is a mother. I am her child. She decides what I do and when. She whispers words I learn to speak. She feeds me—from her alone I am nourished. She may let me cry. But she won't let me die."

Then a million other widows chime in, say things like:

"Your heart will always be broken, but you'll learn to live with it."
And, "Don't think too long or hard about anything."
And, "For a while life becomes something to be endured, not enjoyed."
And, "It never gets any better, but it does get easier."

Then I say:

"Life is a fairy tale, and this is the worst part of the story. We shut our eyes, unsure if we want to keep reading, unsure if we trust this storyteller. But if we close the book now, it will always have a tragic ending. If we stay, it may get worse, it may get better. Grief is staying more than one more minute to see what happens next."

Then the child asks:

"What does 'never' mean?"

I say:

"You think you knew what 'never' meant—but after months of grief, you live it. Grief is finding inside of yourself your *never, nothing, no.*"

Then the child asks:

"Where did Collin go?"

I get down on my knees, wiping tears as I look her straight in the face. "Where do YOU think he went?" I ask.

She pauses. Then says:

"I think he's in the moon and the stars."

—

Seven months after the accident, I go back to work.
My employer gives me a less demanding job, one that spares me from the public eye.
Ten months later I have a breakdown and don't show up for work, go

back on disability for another six months.
I fear I'm permanently damaged.

My first job after *that* is at a butcher shop outside of town. No one there knows me.
I work the 12 hour days like they're nothing.
I like being around the carcasses. They make me feel your death wasn't unusual at all.
Two weeks in, my boss finds out who I am, what happened. He waits until everyone leaves to express his condolences.
I blink back the tears and thank him for his kind words.

—

We're standing on one of the gritty beaches of this world. Erica's pointing upward, telling us, of the albatross that circles: "they're always around… so if we ever need anything to eat…" and your sister lunges just as it lands, white and huge on the sands. "Get it, Zoe!" I cry, and turn my attention back to the waves.

You and I, we're washing our dishes in the salty water. I leave everything behind and walk up to you. Through magnetism wholly, I climb into your arms as you lift me. I feel my skin against your skin, my muscles against your muscles, my blood, warm, against your blood.

"I'm so happy to be with you right now."

"Me too. I'm so thankful for this."

"Every moment…"

"Every flirtation…"

"Every embrace…"

"I am here completely."

"Ready to miss you."
and then, dissolution: me waking up to my other life.

I tell Simone these dreams keep me from letting you go. She stops me, says with a clear, firm voice and tears in her eyes: "Rachel, don't let go of him yet. *Don't you let go of him yet.*"

—

Two years later, the DMV summons me to Binghamton for a "safety and business" hearing about the accident.
It's a bitterly cold winter morning. I'm living in the Catskills now and drive two hours to get there.
Your mom comes and sits by me the whole time.
I don't immediately realize that the nice old people who chat with me in the waiting room and the man who keeps silent in the corner are the ones who hit us, and the man I tried to pass.
In the hearing, I repeat the same version of the events I always have.
When given his turn, the man slowly and firmly contradicts my story.
The old people, their faces pitying and solemn, agree with him.

I go home.
Two months later, the DMV suspends my license for 45 days.
I ride the bus to my job cutting fish at a market.
I don't mind.

—

In a dream, you're making breakfast—an impossible sweetness. You make several dishes. You ask for my advice. I lie in wait and luxury. You are cheerful. I am blessed. (As it was.)

I dreamt of a day with you—the *real* you, riding buses and kissing, almost missing our stop. Holding hands as we sit looking at each other on the sidewalk of Whig Street. Neil takes our picture as a memento I'll get to keep for after you're dead. Though I know that it is imminent—our goodbye—I feel no sadness, just joy at your company and everything we created together.

—

In June of 2017, your parents' petition to the Department of Transportation requesting reevaluation of the passing zone on Route 96 in the Town of Ulysses is granted.

A formal investigation commences, and the town decides to modify the existing pavement markings.

The Regional Traffic Engineer signs a letter informing them of the change. She thanks them, again, for their interest in this matter.

"I'M FINE"

Kelsey Morgenweck

"I'm fine." Two words that got me through most of my early life. People are satisfied with this response. They don't press for more information. I feel safe behind "I'm fine." My vulnerabilities masked for one more conversation.

I'm 4. I'm outside at recess, doing my best to avoid the other kids, as usual. I feel a tightening in my chest and I summon the courage to approach the aide. "My heart hurts," I say. She laughs and pats my head and my anxiety increases. She sends me to the nurse. Another head pat and an "Aww, that's so cute." I hold back tears, struggling to find another way to say it. I don't know what is happening but I know it feels very wrong. My grandma takes me to the doctor. "Asthma," he says. My mother blames herself, so she only continues to smoke for another three years. I adjust. Not being able to breathe becomes normal. I miss a lot of school but I don't mind until I have to go back. My grandma cares for me while my parents work and I feel safe. A classmate points out in front of a group, "Wow, you're sick a lot." I don't know how to respond. I feel ashamed and embarrassed.

I'm 14. I can't get out of bed, but there's a pill for that and I'm relieved. I don't have to talk about what's going on, even though part of me longs to. "SAD." A fitting title for a seemingly appropriate diagnosis.

At 22 I learn that psychiatrists aren't always right, when the medication I've been taking for the past eight years triggers a major manic episode that shakes my core and causes me to doubt my own mind. "Bipolar I." There's a pill for that, too. It takes trying seven before one works. The doctor in the hospital asks, "What does your grandma take?" "For what?" I ask, unaware for 22 years of my genetic legacy. They thought the secrets would keep me safe. "Lithium," my mom informs them. I take four a day and I feel like myself again. My hands shake and my vision is blurred. My body becomes wracked with cystic acne. But I don't care, because there's a pill for that too.

I'm 25. It's a bitterly cold winter, one I am not prepared for. My hands and feet get so cold that it hurts to touch anything. One day I come home from work and, upon removing my winter protection, find my fingers and toes are black and they've lost all feeling but pain. I hop into the shower and the reasonably warm water feels like boiling. I cry out so loudly that my mom comes to check on me. "I'm fine," I say as I sob quietly in the bathtub. "Raynaud's Syndrome." The words feel awkward leaving my mouth and I hate explaining it. I learn to protect myself. To watch for signs that the capillaries are closing. First red. Then tingling. Then white. Then black. I fear winter and I lose trust in my own warmth.

I'm 31. On a hike by myself, as usual. I step down on my right foot and pain explodes from the ball. I soak it in the cold water of the nearby stream and limp out barefoot with my boots hung across my shoulder. "Dancer's toes," the doctor calls it. How could I not have realized that I've been tiptoeing my entire life? It throbs when I walk, but I learn to keep my feet grounded.

I'm 32. I become increasingly aware of a part of my body I've been trying to ignore for 15 years. The hum of pain I've been squashing in the background of my life becomes a scream. Every day I feel it. I agonize. I can't sit and I can't hold my urine. My muscles squeeze my bladder so hard I consider it a good day if I only go every 30 minutes. My body pushes lovers out, even when my mind and voice give an enthusiastic "Yes." "Pelvic floor dysfunction." I've not wanted to acknowledge this pain. I've tried to bury the memory of the injury that left me grateful for my first trauma.

My mind and body know exactly what to do with this pain. I start to talk. I get help. Physical therapy twice a week becomes a routine I find comforting. I learn to relax. I learn to trust my healer and find comfort in her touch. The pain eases and I start thinking clearly. I start to feel again. I experience relief for a few months, but it doesn't last. It's Saturday and I'm at a performance in a church. The cold metal folding chair I'm sitting on ignites a fire inside my body and I shift uncomfortably, struggling to stay still. I worry about blocking the view of the people behind me, about the chair squeaking obnoxiously, and about drawing too much attention to myself as I politely sneak by the other audience members, painfully aware that I wish I didn't have to leave early.

I'm 32. The lithium that's so effectively kept me "healthy" becomes toxic. I'm given no warning as my body begins to cramp like the worst flu I've ever had. I run to the bathroom as waves of nausea rock me. I writhe around on my bed, desperate to end the throbbing in my head. I notice a growing weakness in my arms and legs. I struggle to lift my hands to call 911. I crawl to the door to let in the EMTs. "Do you think you might be having a panic attack?" one of them asks. "No," is all I can muster as they wheel my poisoned body into the ambulance. My signature on the forms reminds me of my grandma's when her Parkinson's acted up. I keep myself calm as I push aside thoughts of stroke. They flush me out. They send me home. I return two more times. I fear dehydration. I doubt my body's ability to filter the drug that saved my life and almost ended it.

I'm 33. I'm bitten by a tick and unknowingly infected with "Lyme." I experience symptoms that can easily be explained by other factors and I wait. I wait a little too long. The underlying issues my body has already been managing come to the surface all at once. The antibiotics erode my stomach lining and it takes two months to balance it. My body aches. I struggle to breathe. To walk. To fight. A part of me just wants to go. To escape. But I get up and heat up some soup because I know no one else will do it for me.

Today it hurts to sit and to lift the growing toddler whose care I'm entrusted with and whom I love so much. My lungs feel heavy and anxiety gnaws at me as I try to relax enough to take a full breath. I'm getting tired of bland chicken and brown rice, but I'm grateful for them when my hunger grows. I've peed so many times I feel like I've lost years of my life and I'm so tired I can't be around anyone. I'm grateful today, though. Yesterday was worse. Tomorrow could be better.

I worry that my physical form will weigh me down and hold me back, but I don't stop taking care of it. I take the pills and try to focus on how they keep me healthy and not how they make me feel sick. I keep going.

Sometimes I wish I didn't have to deal with a body that feels like it's falling apart and a heart that sometimes hurts but keeps on beating. But if anyone asks, "I'm fine."

THE MYSTICAL STORM:
LEARNING TO SURRENDER

Callae Gedrose

In 2013, an electrical storm raged through my brain in the middle of the night.

It was my first grand mal seizure. I had been experiencing partial seizures for a year prior to the grand mal, but they had gone undiagnosed by an emergency room doctor as well as my own physician. My symptoms were ambiguous, so a misinterpretation was inevitable.

Then it happened. The big one. The moment that changed the course of my life and opened the gates to an unimaginable journey of self-discovery.

In the years leading up to the seizures, I had been living from a place of fear, desperation, and resistance. I spent my days fighting to keep my family together and my head above water. It depleted me to the bone. My daily mantra had become, "I just want to disappear."

We must be careful what we ask for. The Universe came knocking and I almost disappeared to the other side. I was stripped down to nothing, gifted with a seizure disorder, and handed everything back with a heart full of knowing.

At some point during the seizure, while my brain was offline, I awakened into a different realm. It was a dream of sorts, but it felt so much more real than our small world of "realities."

I was all-knowing, and free from the density of my body. My ego and sense of self vanished as my consciousness expanded. I felt as vast as the night sky and as small as a speck of dust at the same time. I was connected to everything—stars, earth, humans, animals, plants, and breath. Time felt eternal, yet passed with the snap of a finger. I was shown how our lives resemble a continuum, as we cycle through loops or spirals of time that are all coexisting.

I felt no judgment, fear, or pain. Only peace and love existed in this space. The presence of love was overwhelming and without definition or boundaries—it was a love that doesn't exist in earthly form. I felt as if I were wrapped in the arms of God. Words cannot describe that simultaneous void and fullness of being. I was home.

During this noetic journey, I communicated wordlessly with other entities. I call them "angels," or "spirit guides," for lack of precise description. I asked them what was happening to me. They assured me that I was okay and safe. These angelic voices were many, but spoke in unison. It was the most beautiful sound I have ever heard.

The voices were communicating a series of messages. The first message, which they repeated several times, was, "It's time to start loving yourself."

I resisted. They continued until an understanding came over me that we can only heal each other and our world by healing and loving ourselves first. I was shown repeatedly that we are all one, and how by loving ourselves, we create a powerful ripple effect which, in turn, heals the whole.

I felt myself surrendering to their message and a contract was made with the angels. I had agreed to start loving myself.

The next message was, "You have been given a gift." I don't know what they meant exactly. Was this experience a gift? Are my seizures a gift? Is my life a gift? Or is the telling of my story a gift? Maybe all of these.

The last message they shared was one of gratitude. The angels reminded me of how much I had to be grateful for, especially my family. They showed me images of my boys and my husband. My heart exploded open as I saw how important I was to them.

It was during this final message that I felt the spirit guides gently place their hands on me. I knew that I had to return to my physical existence, my life, and my body.

I slowly began to feel the weight of my body. It felt compressed and painfully dense. I struggled to open my eyes. As I came to, I found that

I had been staring for some time at a large etching on the wall next to me. I realized I was back in this world.

I felt warm tears streaming down my face. I longed to find a way back to the bliss I had been engulfed in moments before. I closed my eyes and prayed for the angels to take me back. I was willing to leave my life and my family to return to the infinite love of a higher consciousness. Despite my pleas, I found myself right back where I started, seizures and all.

At first I was afraid to share my experience, for fear of being labeled crazy or delusional. It took me two years to find the courage to tell my neurologist. I thought he would offer a clear and logical explanation for how the firing of the neurons in my brain during my seizure had manufactured this experience. Instead, he told me he couldn't offer a scientific explanation, and that he believed I'd had a near death or mystical experience.

His words were like salve to my soul. He gave me the validation I needed to intellectually accept what I knew in my heart to be true.

I'm still working to uphold my contract with the angels. This human being business is hard. I'm not always kind and loving toward myself. It's a constant practice.

One of the greatest lessons my seizure disorder and mystical awakening have taught me is surrender. Surrender can be a difficult task, requiring disciplined contemplation and self-reflection, unless you're faced with circumstances that leave no other options.

Fortunately for me, learning surrender was spontaneous. It was like instantly uncovering a long-buried treasure that might never have been found without the storms raging in my brain. I couldn't fight, or deny, or run after being stripped down to my bare bones. I was forced to face my circumstances and let go.

To me, surrender is placing my heart and soul in the hands of grace as I free-fall. It is an explicit decision to release my scattered uncertainty over to something greater than myself, trusting that there is a larger process at play than I can possibly imagine. Surrendering is not giving up or resigning. It's accepting what *is* without judgment or attachment. It includes embracing fear, misguided perception, and all that is outside of my control.

Surrender has been the key to dissolving resistance and finding patience, perseverance, and resilience within myself. To me, resistance is temporary struggle encapsulated in self-abandonment. The moment I humbly surrender is the moment I reclaim my power and reignite my inner flame. Surrender is the return to our pristine and eternal existence. Surrender is freedom. Surrender is peace.

I don't think I needed to have seizures or a near-death experience to awaken to the love that I am, that we all are. All I had to do was drop in and stop fighting myself. For years I believed that I was broken to the core, but now I finally see the beauty in all of my shortcomings, as well as my strengths. How can I be anything but grateful for where this path has led me?

I believe the Universe meets us in the places we least expect it to. It will come to us on its own terms and with a very distinct purpose. It doesn't need our permission, it doesn't conform to our agenda, and it certainly won't tolerate our resistance. It only seeks our surrender.

CUTTING MY LOSSES, WITH HELP FROM LITTLE MOTHER ELDER TREE

Audrey Gilbert

I didn't think I wanted a third baby. I was still healing from the wounds of young single motherhood. I had already spent most of my adult life as a devoted, nurturing mother, and while I loved my two kids beyond words, I was ready to do other things. I treasured my creative time away from my children like scraps of bread I had to hoard and eat in secret, lest someone snatch them away. I had fought hard to find time apart from my caregiving duties to kindle a few personal passions, and the flames were just starting to hold. I feared another child would quench them completely and I would be "nothing but a mother" my whole life. So it wasn't entirely pure joy I felt when I discovered we had conceived again. When I saw the pink line on the stick, I cried.

I wasn't ready to make a decision yet, so I let a couple of weeks pass in ambiguity. But as the days turned into nights, I started to fall gently in love with the idea of this third baby. I began to dream sweet dreams about the little one, from which I would rise and wonder: *Could I bring another child into the world?* I had to admit that it was a good time to do it. My second was still little. I still had all the baby gear. This third baby, more than either of the others, could anticipate a stable home and healthy family when she arrived. We had a safe place to live. I had a supportive, loving, patient partner who loved being a father. We were a happy family, for the most part.

And so, despite the mixed emotions, a sense of hope began to prevail. By week 13, we had already picked out the name Juniper. I knew this was my last chance to experience the magic of birth and baby-rearing, and I was ready. We joked about the need to "round out the family" with one more.

It was almost week 14 when we finally got the appointment for our first exam. My first two babes had been born at home, but this time would be different. I had decided that I wanted to labor in a birthing center, being that we lived in a communal housing situation that didn't have a lot of privacy. I also wanted a bit more pampering the third time around than a home birth could deliver. We arrived at the birthing center's medical office fully committed and totally excited to hear our baby's heartbeat for the first time.

It happened right as the slimy lubricant jelly was rubbed on my belly and the fetal monitor was turned on. I suddenly had this feeling. A cold, grey feeling spread through the room. It felt like time slowed down. The doctor was talking and smiling, but I couldn't hear him. A voice spoke in my head with stark clarity, *There is no heartbeat.* I did not feel afraid, but I did not like the cold grey that was spreading over my limbs and heart. Still, I just knew. I waited for the doctor to confirm what I knew. He avoided my eyes. He tried again and again, from one position and the next, reassuring us each time that this didn't mean anything definite. He ordered an ultrasound. The ultrasound technician wasn't allowed to give us any answers, so we drove home and waited for the doctor's final diagnosis. We waited for hours just to confirm what I had already understood in my body: the baby was no longer alive. It was a dark, gloomy, cold March day. The new moon was a couple of days away, as was the equinox. We cried and lay in bed side by side. No one knew what else to do. When the doctor finally did call, he was apologetic, offering, "Sometimes these things just happen." And he was right. They just do.

———

The days spent waiting for my body to release the would-be-baby were the worst. They seemed to drag on forever. How strange it is to have a dead baby inside your body. I tried not to think about it, but more and more the fantasy of the little person inside was changing into a nightmare, like a parasite or a ghoul in my womb. I tried to cry, but mostly I felt numb and in-between. There was nothing to mourn yet, except my hopes and expectations. I drank cupfuls of 'healthy cycle' tea, hoping to hasten the process, but those puny little tea bags weren't cutting it. Ironically, many of the plants in the blend are also uterine tonics, repackaged and sold as the 'pregnancy tea' I was drinking a week earlier. At this time, I didn't know much about emmenagogues. If I had had the counsel of a wise woman then, she might have helped me reach for something stronger, like parsley, angelica, or blue cohosh. But I didn't have the energy for research. I didn't want to try at all.
My instinct was to hide away. So I lay in bed and went inward, calling out for guides and plant spirits to help me. Each time I found my way

to inner stillness, I saw an Elder tree spirit waiting for me there. She knew the heavy heart I dragged with me, and she understood like a grandmother who has seen it all. She understood because she existed in between, where death and life are one. She offered a place by her roots for me to bury the placenta and the blood. Blood, marrow, womb tissue as it both grows and molts. These are her languages, her tools. She would care for them. *Leave it to me. Come, child, let go.*

The cramps finally came 8 days after the news of the dead fetus. Shedding it was so much more painful than the "heavy period" they said it would feel like. In the movies, miscarriage usually goes like this: an unsuspecting pregnant couple is asleep peacefully in bed when the mother-to-be is awoken by a sudden pain. She cries out and is surprised to find a heavy blood flow. It's over. She cries. Sad music plays. In real life, I had hours of cramping and contracting with a slow drip of blood. I camped out in the bathroom, moaning and gripping the toilet seat, waiting. Once in a while a thick clot would slip out. My husband sat near me, worried. He wanted to help but had no power to take away the pain. It wasn't unlike real labor, except that there was no crowning moment, no final courageous push, and no instant relief and bliss at the end. All that was left for my efforts was a toilet bowl full of bloody mess. When the pains finally stopped around 1:00 in the morning, I was spent.

But what now? What do I do with this bloody mess? I had imagined burying her under an elder tree, as my vision had suggested. I had imagined a ceremony, a song, with candles, hand-holding, and tears. But now that it came to it, I was too exhausted, frustrated, and to be frank, a little annoyed with the whole process. *What a waste!* was the only thing going through my mind. I thought about trying to scoop out the clots from the toilet bowl to bury them in the earth, but I was too freaked and grossed out to put my hands in there. I could not discern what was me and what was baby, and I could not bear to scoop out masses of uterine tissue from the soupy toilet mess. So I just flushed it. There was nothing glamorous or spiritual about it. Like a dead pet fish, gone down the pipes.

—

Grief is so much more complicated than I thought it would be. Sure, there is sadness and pain. But for me, it was mixed with relief, bitterness, and shame. I was torn apart with sorrow for the loss of this charming little one. I was resentful that she had stayed just long enough to win me over, and annoyed with myself for being lulled into unrequited love by false dreams. I was bitter at the disappointment of what could no longer be. I felt foolish for having said yes to the idea of welcoming her into my arms in the first place. But I was also relieved to be given a free pass from the years of work required to nurture a child. Yes, it's true: I was happy to be free of it. I was off the hook. How can all of these things be true at once? And how do you express these conflicting truths in a way that anyone can understand?

I struggled to process my loss. I wanted to talk about it, but I didn't know what to say. It didn't seem like the kind of thing people talked about. What do you do when you're needing emotional support, but no one can support you in the way you need? I reached out to a few people, but their responses were mostly awkward. "You are young, you can have another," well-intentioned people suggested. But it wasn't another baby I wanted. Was it? No, not another baby. I didn't know what I wanted. Maybe I had wanted just this? Maybe I had unconsciously willed the miscarriage to come to pass? I *did* know that I didn't want to hear anyone else tell me, "But you'll try again!" Not ever again, please.

I suppose the worst part was the aversion I felt toward my own body. I felt horrified and ashamed of its egregious failure. It had let us all down. My uterus and I were not on good terms. I was a hollow, barren, child-loser, rotten with unfulfilled promise. Full of death. A sickly smelling squash, rotting on the vine.

It's an interesting word, miscarriage. It implies a mistake. Like you've dropped something out of carelessness. Like a raw egg has slipped out of your hands and shattered on the tile floor because you were moving too quickly. As if there were a group of people circling around you, laughing and singing that nursery rhyme, "A tisket a tasket, you dropped your little basket."

—

I spent more time in bed that week, drinking tea and reading to distract myself. I turned to fairy tales, which so often speak to what is otherwise unspeakable: vicious loss and tragedy, as well as wondrous miracles and joy. Fairy tales are full of orphaned children without guidance or resources, who somehow make it through unimaginable hardships. I am always inspired by them. This time, I happened to find a story by Hans Christian Anderson called *The Little Elder-Tree Mother*. It's a story about a boy who is sick in bed. His mother makes him a pot of elderflower tea, and while it's steeping, the boy watches the steam rise out of the pot. He sees it take the shape of an elder tree, which then morphs into a friendly granny, and then into a kindly old man and old woman who reminisce about the happy times in their lives. They recall when they first fell in love, their wedding day, and before then, when they were children happily playing in the branches of an elder tree. The old woman tells a story about a time of separation, when she thought she had lost her love, and then of their joyful reunion beside the elder tree. The boy is comforted and soothed by the vision, and when he wakes, he doesn't know if it was real, or if he had been dreaming.

For some reason, this story made me weep the kind of tears I had been needing to weep. I felt comforted by the image of Little-Elder-Mother. She was the wise, old grandmother I wished I had to lean on. I knew I had some elderflower stocked in my pantry, so I made a pot of elder tea, all the while letting my tears flow. I got back into bed and did what the sick boy in the story had done: I watched the steam until I dreamed of my own loss and separation from the life I had been preparing to welcome home, and of a joyful reunion with her under the flexible boughs of the Elder mother, whose branches were like arms wrapped around us.

———

When I look back at that time, I still feel the ache of confused, unnamed, unshared loss. The loss of the dream of my baby was just the first of several devastating disappointments that year, the first domino in a chain reaction of mini-deaths. A few months after the miscarriage, I quit my job. Then, the cooperative living and farming project I was involved in began to unravel, and with it all of my hopes and dreams and security of home. The theme of that year of my life was *miscarriage*. I struggled with my feelings of failure as the losses and false starts kept coming. Why couldn't I do anything right? But Elder-Mother reminded me: *let it go. I will hold it for you*. It was a year of painful goodbyes, each one as complicated and conflicted as the first. But each time I surrendered and let go, space opened up inside, along with stillness and peace. I learned the term *ambiguous loss*, and I held onto it like a worry stone, until I didn't need it anymore.

What does acceptance mean, really? Adjusting to the reality that so much is beyond my control has always been hard for me. Truth be told, having to come to terms with miscarriage, both literally and symbolically, has helped me discern the difference between what I can control and what I can't. I've become a lot better at cutting my losses, so to speak. By the first anniversary of the loss of my baby, we were finally cutting our ties with our failed business and uprooting our family for another move. I let some unhealthy relationships go. It was painful. Sad. Confusing. But it was time. I trusted myself more, having been through the pain of miscarriage. I knew we would come out the other side.

We bought our first house, tucked deep in the Catskill Mountains, sheltered by tall oaks and maples and pines. Inspired by my experience with elder, I began an herbal mentorship program that perfectly aligned with my needs and desires. The name of the school was Elder Moon School of Herbal Medicine. How's that for synchronicity? A week before the second anniversary of the date we got our sad news from the doctor, I found an elder tree growing along the roadside, just a quarter of a mile down the street from our house.

I never did have the ceremony that I imagined under the elder branches to mark my loss and lay it to rest. But whenever I pass this elder tree, I bow and blow a kiss to my little child—the one who laughs while playing in the Little Elder Mother's branches. Sometimes, when I feel lonely or sad, I bring little shiny coins, fresh baked bread, or sweet tea to my neighborhood elder tree and leave them at the base of her roots. I have come to understand Elder-Mother as a keeper of lost memories—past and future—and as a guardian of lost and sick children. To me, she stands guard at the gates of death and rebirth. If you ask her, she might lift the veil for you too, and show you the reunion or homecoming your heart has been longing for.

DAVE

Lynn Myles

He was funny and playful.
He journaled daily. He was smart.
He was a poet and photographer.
He worked on Capitol Hill for a senator, and got our family passes to the White House.
I sometimes called him my uncle, but he wasn't really. Not a cousin, either, really.
He was my first cousin Mandy's husband.
She was 10 years older than me. He was 8 years older than her.
I was in their wedding party in 1972. A junior bridesmaid, at age 9. I wore my first pair of pantyhose.
The whole family loved him.
In some ways, he was the father I never had.
In other ways, he was like a big brother.
Mandy and Dave took my younger brother and me to Kings Dominion.
He taught us how to speak in code with "Charlie Oscar Delta Echo."
He played Wiffle ball with us when we visited my aunt and uncle in Alexandria.
He took us to our first concert ever, The Beach Boys.

Thanksgiving was our big family holiday.
"Over the River and Through the Woods" to Mamaw and Papaw's house we'd go.
Watching my brother and me try to give each other back rubs one Thanksgiving, Dave taught us the basics of Swedish massage. Lessons I carry to this day.

We're a touchy family.
Of course everyone got hugs and embraces.
Family gatherings always include back scratches, shoulder rubs, and foot massages.
My aunt, a beauty consultant, even gave us facial massages. My mom trained in reflexology.
We'd all sit around the living room, talking and laughing, stroking and

touching.

Touch was easy and natural.

At some point, the nature of the touches changed with Dave.
Gentle caresses on my palm, his fingers playing on mine.
A hand on my back. A stroke on my arm.
Hidden, of course. But often. I knew they weren't quite right.
The thing was, I loved the extra attention.
Someday, I'd be lucky enough to have a husband like him.
He believed in "women's lib" and pulled his weight with the housework.
He was so good with their baby girl.
He told stories. He suggested books I should read.
He was kind to everyone. He made us all laugh.

When I was 13, Mom, my brother and I made our biennial trip from
Ohio to Alexandria to stay with my aunt and uncle. Mandy and Dave
lived nearby in Falls Church with their 2-year-old.
Mom had planned for us to then visit Mamaw and Papaw and come
back a couple of weeks later.
I asked to stay.
To stay with Mandy and Dave.
To help take care of my 2-year-old cousin.
To stretch my wings.
To experience the bicentennial in Washington, D.C.

It was July 4, 1976 in the nation's capital. I felt so lucky!
Anticipation mounted as we planned how we would see the fireworks
that night.
We weren't crazy enough to fight the crowds downtown.
Based on rumors, we joined others on a hill in Arlington, certain we'd
be able to see.
But as they started, we could only see reflected light against the clouds.
No sparks. No oohs and ahhs.
The lawn chairs folded up and people sheepishly walked back to their
cars.
I tried to mask my disappointment.
I held in my tears until we got back,
until I had brushed my teeth,
until I was in my room.

Maybe he heard me crying, or maybe he would have come anyway.

He walked into the dark room, held out his arms, and said, "Come here."

I got out of bed. His arms wrapped around me. I needed to be held.

My teary cheek rested against his t-shirt.

But then he lifted my chin and kissed me. A real kiss. A kiss with tongue. Invading. Shocking.

What was I supposed to do? I'd never had a kiss like that before.

I tried to kiss back. Was that what he wanted?

He left. I couldn't sleep.

Early the next morning, I sat in the living room in my pajamas. Thinking. Staring into space.

He came down before Mandy was awake, leaned over, and kissed me again. His hand rested on top of my thigh. His thumb stroked across the line.

I can't remember the details of the next days and weeks. I don't remember how many caresses happened, or how many times his fingers trespassed over parts of my clothing.

I do remember that at some point, my mom came back and we went to my aunt's house for the rest of our stay. Mandy and Dave stayed at my aunt's for the weekend, too. That way there could be more family time.

One night, just after dinner, I took a shower. Everyone else was downstairs watching TV.

As I was drying off, Dave opened the bathroom door, slipped in, and closed the door behind him.

I froze. My throat closed up. My towel felt inadequate.

He spoke gently. He reached out and stroked my breasts. His hand slipped between my legs.

He kissed me. I tried to kiss back.

But I was still frozen, frightened.

"Do you want to touch me?" he asked as he unzipped.

No, I didn't. But I couldn't say a word.

He held it out for me to touch. It was big and ugly. I stroked it a couple of times with one finger, like you might a bird.

I'd never seen a man's penis before. Just my little brother's, and he was still a boy.

I wanted it to go away.

He didn't stay long. I waited until I couldn't hear anything in the hall and went back to the guest room to get dressed. About 15 minutes later, he came to the bedroom and knocked. I said he could come in.
"I'm sorry," he said. "That shouldn't have happened. If you need to tell your mom or someone, you can. I just don't know what would happen. It would cause a lot of pain."

So I kept it a secret.
I didn't want to be responsible for tearing apart the family or my cousin's marriage. My mom had once said that if anyone ever molested me, that she would hunt them down and castrate them. What would my mom do to Dave? He wasn't just "someone," he was the family favorite.
And wasn't I partly to blame? I knew the touching wasn't right, but I didn't know how to stop it and still keep the extra attention I got from this special man.

Life continued on as "normal." Over the next few years, I sometimes received more-than-family touches from Dave. But never another kiss. Never another bathroom invasion. The touching eventually stopped.

In 1981, just before I started college, Dave and I talked about it briefly. I can't remember what he said exactly. Something about me being special. All I remember saying was, "But I was just a little girl…"

The story stayed locked inside. No one knew.
Not the husband I married in 1985. Not any of my friends. Certainly not my mother.
Thanksgiving continued to be our family's favorite holiday.
Dave made us laugh around the dinner table. We all shared stories of church and family life. There were still back rubs. The kids all played. Mandy and Dave had five children. My husband and I had three.

In 1997, Mandy and Dave split up. They had seemed so good together. Mandy went off with some other man.

In the fall of 1997, Mandy asked to meet with me. I'd just started seminary. She explained a few of her reasons for wanting to leave Dave.

Despite their five children, Dave had a very low libido, she said, and she wasn't satisfied.

And then she abruptly said, "Tell me about the abuse."
"What do you mean?"
"When you were a little girl. That summer you stayed with us. He told me about the night in the bathroom."
It took me a while to understand what she meant.
"When did he tell you?" I asked.
"That very same night."

She knew. She had known.
I had been alone with my secret for over 20 years, afraid it would hurt her too much if she knew. But she had known all along.
Was it abuse? Is that what I'd call it?

I told her my story. But not the part about me liking the extra attention. She told me she could tell that he liked younger girls. It was probably why he'd been attracted to her in the first place. It was probably also why his libido was low with her later. She said she had been vigilant during her girls' sleepovers, suspicious. She didn't know of anyone else he had touched. Could we know?

Part of me was relieved. The secret was out.
Part of me was angry. Why hadn't she spoken up?

But she had only been 24. The mother of a two-year-old girl. She had quit her job as a secretary when she had her baby. She was frightened. What would she do if she lost her husband?

She had hoped that the story would come out without having to ask me about it. She thought it would have happened during my intense psychological screening for ordination. But no, that secret was locked away. I had managed it just fine in its box. Now that box was open.

In the days that followed, I told my husband, my bishop, a therapist, my best girlfriends, my mom... and then, bit by bit, the rest of the family. The short version, at least.

Soon afterward, Dave asked to meet. I don't know what either of us were expecting. Were we trying to find some sort of reconciliation? He acknowledged the sadness of his breakup with Mandy. How much he loved his kids. He said that he didn't have a thing for young girls, that there had never been anyone else.

He said, "It wasn't just my fault. You came on to me."

I felt disgusted.

In talking about my path in seminary, he told me that he, too, had thought about being an Episcopal priest.

I felt like throwing up.

Until that year, I had never processed my story as an adult. It had stayed locked away in my 13-year-old brain.

I began to hear my friends' and therapist's words:

"It wasn't your fault. He was the adult."

"How dare they let a little girl hold this secret for the whole family."

"You think you flirted? Of course you flirted! It's what tween-age girls do! Girls test out their emerging womanhood with safe men in their families. A good man affirms the girl, models healthy boundaries, and never crosses them."

"When you were 13, he was 31. And it started when you were 11."

I found a way to integrate the story into my life. I felt surprisingly undamaged.

Thanksgivings changed. That was probably inevitable.

I only heard from Dave one more time. He sent a card to my church address shortly after I divorced and moved in 2012.

He is still a good writer. He said he was sad for my sadness. He reflected on how unpredictable life could be. He invited me to reach out to him.

The card sat on my desk for three days before I threw it away.

THE LETTER

Katy McGrann

"I'm checking my email one last time," I say to my husband, Dave, as he goes out to retrieve the snail mail.

I'm about to head out for a weekend dance and yoga retreat, and I'm on a tight schedule to meet my carpool friends. Dave and I will just have time for a quick hug and kiss before I head out the door.

"Do you know someone in Bristow, Virginia?" he asks.

I search my brain bank. No addresses come to mind. "Not that I can remember," I reply.

"Well, you got a certified letter, and that's never good," he says as he hands it over.

I rip open the letter, quickly and carelessly, certain that it's a scam of some sort. Until I see two phrases: "January 22, 1982" and "Ohio Valley Medical Center."
I drop it on the kitchen counter as tears start to form.
After a pause, Dave asks, "Certified letter … is it her?"

—

In April, almost 39 years ago, I celebrated my 21st birthday a bit too exuberantly and became pregnant. In the middle of October, my parents whisked me away from college in Richmond, VA, to a Florence Crittenton Home in Wheeling, WV. For the next three months, I lived with 20 or so troubled girls trying to figure out how to deal with my own shame, which paled in comparison to the trauma experienced by many of the girls I met there.

My family concocted a backstory for why I was leaving school: there was a crisis at home. In fact, there was a crisis at home. That's another long, painful story, intertwined with my own, about my dad cheating on my mom and leaving home at the same time I was pregnant. Because of all of that, we lied. The story was that I was going to live with my great-aunt in North Carolina to deal with the trauma of the trouble.

My family, God bless them, did all they could to include me in our usual Thanksgiving and Christmas traditions. Everyone—parents, siblings, grandparents, aunts and uncles, and a very few trusted family friends—knew about my indiscretion. Under the cover of darkness, they all helped as "look-outs" to bring me home from Crittendon for the usual holiday celebrations. It seems absurd now, but it really was like a James Bond affair; I'd sneak through the garage or the back door and stay quiet upstairs during parties or when visitors stopped by. Just surreal.

The following January, I gave birth to a beautiful baby on my best friend's birthday, with my mom and one of my sisters by my side. My mom said she had seen a double rainbow that day, so she knew everything was going to be okay. I placed my baby girl up for adoption to loving parents three or four days later, and my mom was with me when I signed the papers. We both cried the whole way home. I was 21 years old. To this day, it was the hardest decision I've ever made.

I had always said that if she ever found me, I would welcome her with arms wide open, and so would my family. Through the wonders of DNA testing, she did. When that certified letter came in the mail, I found out her name is Jennifer. She asked if I was her birth mother, and if I was willing to share family health information. "I don't want to cause you any pain," Jennifer wrote, "but I would like to learn more about you and my birth family."

I replied to her letter with a long email, sent with some trepidation, telling her more about us and inviting her to connect, if she was up for it. This past spring, Jennifer and her husband traveled to Richmond to visit. As they pulled into our driveway, my heart pounded and my eyes puddled up. When we hugged, all of my anxiety melted away.

I'm so happy to have spent time with her and her husband and to share some family stories, to have her meet her half-sister and my husband, and to know she hopes to meet her half-brother soon. That afternoon we were all grateful that everything felt "normal and lovely," as one family member put it. We felt ready to see where this journey would lead us.

The family members who were there through my pregnancy and her birth are ecstatic. They have held her in their hearts for as long as I have and can't wait to meet her and her family. I didn't share this story publicly until the "daughter that I waited to find me" and the "daughter that I raised myself" both shared it on social media. The minute the two of them did, I wrote a Facebook post, not caring how many of my friends, my mother's friends, my siblings' friends, or my "friends of friends" saw it.

I have been waiting for over 38 years to release this secret to the world. It's a relief and a blessing.
And, thanks be to God, it's not a secret anymore.

A SECRET FROM MYSELF

Deirdre Silverman

There are secrets we keep from others, and secrets we keep from ourselves: ones that are so painful or dangerous that we erase them from our memory.

Throughout most of high school in the 1960's, I was in love with a boy named Billy. We had very little in common, but there was a strong passionate pull between us, exacerbated by our raging adolescent hormones. We were afraid to have sex, or at least I was, so we'd date for a while, make each other crazy with desire, and then break up when we couldn't stand the tension anymore. The next year we'd get back together and repeat the process.

When I was 15, I decided to make Billy jealous by going out with one of his close friends. None of them was as handsome, smart, athletic, or in any other way as desirable as Billy, but they were close enough to him to have some appeal to me. And they were all interested in me, since they'd been watching the ups and downs of our passion for some time. So one summer, I made a date with Mark.

On the night of our date, I was also invited to a party at my friend Amy's house. She and her family were among the more intellectual and eccentric people in our suburban town, and I knew that Mark was much too dumb and coarse for her party. He and I had made plans to go to the beach, but my parents wouldn't allow that. So I told them I was going to Amy's party and left the house with my bathing suit under my clothes.

That night, the beach clubs that lined the Atlantic were closed and deserted. So we drove into one of the parking lots, jumped the fence, went swimming and made out on the beach. Although I didn't really like Mark, it was exciting to be alone together on the dark beach. It felt as though we had the whole ocean to ourselves. But if I wasn't going to have sex with Billy, I certainly wasn't going to do much with Mark. After a while, we headed back to the parking lot, but when Mark lifted himself up to jump the fence, he saw a police car parked next to his.

What could we do? We waited to see if the cop would leave, but he didn't. It was getting late. I had to be home and it was cold, so we had to do something. Mark ran to the next beach club and used a payphone to call his friends, but he couldn't reach anyone. He left messages saying they should come get us. We waited a while longer but they didn't come. Feeling that we had no other choice, we went back over the fence to face the cop.

After bawling us out and threatening to arrest us for trespassing, the cop told Mark to wait in his car and had me get in the patrol car. He started questioning me about what had happened on the beach. What had Mark and I done together? Where had he touched me? Had I taken off the top of my bathing suit? The questions became more specific and persistent, and there was a strange urgency in his voice. Then he said, "Oh Christ, look at this. Now what am I going to do?" I looked towards him and saw that his pants were unzipped and his erect penis was sticking up. It was the first adult penis I had ever seen.

I was shocked, but I was also curious to see what it looked like. Then he said, "I can't go home like this. You have to help me out here," and I realized I was in big trouble. He wanted me to jerk him off, or something worse. I started to cry. While the tears were real, for some reason I also started to tell a story that had no basis in fact and got more elaborate as it went on. I told him my father had a heart condition that prevented him from working and we didn't know how we would pay for college, so I had to maintain a good record to get scholarships, if I got into trouble it would kill him, on and on I went. I was blubbering and lying, and the combination must have punctured his lust because after a while he let me go. I got back into Mark's car and just after that, Billy and the other guys arrived.

They were all in the car as we drove to my house. I didn't say a word to any of them. I just curled up in the corner of the back seat, in shock over what had happened. When Billy asked why I had been in the police car for so long, and why I was crying, I said nothing. I knew I couldn't tell anyone about it. I wasn't supposed to be on the beach. I was supposed to be at Amy's party. I shouldn't have been with Mark at all.

No one would believe that we didn't have sex. The cop was a respected policeman, probably married with kids. I was a bad girl. Who would believe me? I felt filthy.

My sister lived in the beach town where this happened. From time to time I saw the cop there, and each time he gave me a big smile. I was always afraid of him. Once, when my family and I went to a diner in town, he was sitting at the counter. He turned on his stool and winked at me. My parents didn't notice, but I was unable to eat. I kept all of this a secret from everyone, even from Billy when we got back together in September and he wanted to know what happened that night. When I left for college, I made what happened a secret from myself as well. I put it out of my mind, and "forgot" about it for more than ten years.

In my late 20's, I taught Sociology and Women's Studies. In my classes, we read about and discussed sexual harassment and assault. One day, while talking to my husband and a couple of female students, the memory of what happened that night suddenly came back to me and I told them my story. I wasn't sure where the memory had come from, or where it had been, because I hadn't thought of it once in all those years. I think perhaps I kept it a secret until I had the tools I needed to forgive myself. I've never forgiven the cop.

"WHY DON'T WE TAKE OFF OUR CLOTHES?"
ONE MAN'S JOURNEY TOWARD HEALING

Anonymous

"Why don't we take off our clothes…?" suggested the priest, in more of a coaxing directive than a question. "I'll throw them in the dryer, it'll just take a few minutes."

We had just gotten soaked running from the car to the rectory in a rainstorm, after swimming, playing racquetball, and showering at the Y. Why had he parked so far away from the front door in a downpour, when there were plenty of spots closer?

Watching him pull the white plastic clergy collar out from the neckline lapels of his black shirt always struck me as such an intimate act, and a signal portending some kind of vulnerability ahead. Little did I know what he had in mind.

I met this priest at a youth retreat when he was still a deacon, and was 'groomed' over the course of four years before this incident happened. Over the years he had wooed me with playful attention in the swimming pool, on the racquetball court, and in the YMCA sauna. Although I had noticed his eyes looking at my genital area when we were in the locker room, I brushed it off and discounted it. After the periodic sports competitions when he'd alternately praise and tease me, he'd take me to Friendly's for a banana split, or back to the rectory for chocolate cake. Sometimes we would pray together in a private room, making it normal to be alone together. He was always very affectionate, holding my head in his hands, kissing me on the forehead before or after a prayer. I attended his ordination when he was made a priest, and he kissed me on the face in the parking lot. Another time, when he visited me at my house and was saying goodbye, he casually kissed me on the lips and then made it seem like it hadn't happened. I made an excuse and bolted for the house, confused about what had just occurred.

So on this day, after four years of being ensnared by his special attention, I had driven to his parish in another town. We played racquetball as usual, showered off, and swam in the Y pool. Afterward we sat in the sauna nude, which he had normalized over the years, all the while staring at my groin area frequently. When we drove back to the rectory, it was pouring rain, but for some reason he parked at the far end of the lot, so we had to run to get under cover. We were soaked and went up to his quarters, which again had been normalized for the housekeeping staff since we had met and prayed in a 'counseling' room up there before (why it had a twin bed, along with a desk and chair, I'll never know).

This time he suggested that we change out of our clothes. He offered to throw them in the dryer and loan me a bathrobe, which would obviously be way too big. I agreed, since heck, we'd been nude in the locker room earlier in the day, although that was public and this was a very, very private space. I sat on the bed in the counseling room, and for some reason he took quite a while before coming back (looking back, I think he was praying that he wouldn't act on his impulses).

Once back in the room, he sat next to me, mentioned how special I was in God's eyes, and talked about things like what my name meant in Hebrew. He asked if I had any questions about God or my personal, spiritual, or interestingly enough, physical development (puberty came on very late for me). Then he leaned over and took my head in his hands. He slowly pushed me backward on the bed, and started French kissing me while laying on top of me. I was petrified. I had never even kissed a girl, much less French kissed anyone, so I had only heard about this. It was clear he had a full erection through his robe and he moved his hand to my groin to see if I was being turned on, which I wasn't. He then put his hand under my butt and pushed his finger into the hole there. I just froze. Should I scream and make a scene? I just tried to survive it.

It felt like forever, but was probably just ten minutes of him groping. When it was clear he wasn't getting the response he had hoped for, he sat up, pulled me up, and asked if I wanted to pray with him. Without any response from me, he started praying, thanking God for our special relationship and saying that I was a child of God and that it was okay to be close like that. When he was done he asked if I had any questions. What the hell was I supposed to say? He got our clothes and walked me downstairs past the housekeeper as if what just happened was the most normal thing in the world. I wondered: "Could she tell? Did she even suspect?" My whole mind and body were on such high alert that I thought it would be obvious to anyone, but since priests were held in such high esteem, she probably didn't notice anything awry.

The amazing part is that I kept meeting with him a few times a year, wherever he was serving a parish, up until a few months before I was married. How could I have been so under his thrall?

I'm now 62, and was raised Catholic. I was raised on innocence. In my big Catholic family, there was never any mention of our bodies, emotional closeness or intimacy of any kind, and certainly not sex. Looking back, I suspect I was unconsciously looking for a father figure.

We had moved from the Midwest to a college town in the east when I was 10, and I stepped into Catholic school in the middle of the year. After 8th grade, I went to public school and was a 'goody-two-shoes'—even becoming 'Principal for a Day.' I only had one girlfriend in high school and never did anything more than "HH" (holding hands) for fear that kissing would lead to anything sexual, which was never discussed—in my world at least. I got involved in Boy Scouts and heard lots of phrases loaded with sexual innuendo, but half the time didn't fully understand the references. The same occurred with sports teams I was on: lots of banter and teasing but no real information. The only sex-ed film I ever saw was in Catholic school, when the boys were separated from the girls and we watched a movie with diagrams but no human bodies. On a class trip in 8th grade I told some of the guys I knew where babies came from: kissing.

While I didn't have a lot of friends growing up (I played mostly with my siblings), the alleyway was the neighborhood gathering spot, and from there we could easily see into each other's backyards. I remember once seeing one of the neighbor boys playing catch with his dad. I marveled at them, thinking how odd it was to see a dad like that, while also feeling a yearning jealousy.

So from age 15 to 24, I was groomed and abused by this perpetrator priest, who saw my innocence and coveted it, for his own private pleasure. How could I have tolerated that treatment for so many years without stopping it somehow, and how did it affect me afterward? I don't smoke, drink, do drugs, surf porn, eat or work to excess. Of course I have idiosyncrasies, but by all outward signs I've had a successful life. I've acted out in small and large ways, but generally in an 'under-the-radar' manner, essentially giving the finger to the world privately, which often undermined my own aspirations. Yet not a day goes by without some of those images and experiences haunting me, especially when I'm scared, angry, sad, or bored. They imprinted on my mind in ways I can never be rid of.

How can I ever possibly describe the huge impact this had on my life?

It's been 47 years since I first met that priest, and to this day, the hardest part about being abused and molested by him was the 'mind-fuck.' I was so groomed that he got inside my head. I somehow tolerated the leering, the voyeurism, and the exhibitionism that eventually led up to the sexual abuse. As an insecure boy, he gave me such adulation and adoration that I minimized the cost he required for the attention, being nude in front of him on hundreds of occasions for his perverted pleasure.

To this day I can't change clothes, pee, shower, see myself in mirrors, or be in locker rooms without having those images of him gazing at me and showing his nudity to me pop into my head. As a teen when he looked at me in the nude, I wondered if he could tell that I masturbated. Perversely, some of my fantasies began to include him looking at me, wanting me. How can you kick out a hurtful set of experiences and searing images that have parked themselves inside your head?

Years after I married, he stopped by my home when I wasn't there and chatted with my wife, who knew who he was and kept him out in the yard, far away from our children. It was clear that he still carried a perverted videotape in his mind that he played over and over for his enjoyment. It was years later that I learned he engaged in the same 'MO' (down to the exact same phrases) with dozens of boys after me.

I have worked with numerous treatment modalities over the years: clinical psychologists, male and female therapists using different techniques (behavioral therapy, emotive therapy, EMDR, hypnosis, etc.), support groups for survivors (both mixed-gender and all-male), shamanic consultation, guided visualizations, homeopathy, and all different kinds of bodywork. I consider myself lucky that I have been able to use all of these resources throughout my healing journey, and hope that agencies and public policy advocates can continue to make them available to survivors and their families and relationships, to break the cycle of abuse for future generations.

I have raised four daughters and have generally chosen to work part-time, so I can stay close to them throughout their lives and be able to notice any nuanced changes in their behavior. They know about my abuse and I'm sure it has affected their relationships, as it has affected my own. I know I sit on a volcano of anger, and beneath that, deep grief about the loss of innocence and broken trust. I've learned to suppress any strong feelings so I won't overreact. I still have a sweet tooth as a way to 'stuff' the feelings. I wear baggy pants, double swimsuits, and well-worn clothes, so no one will have a chance to be a voyeur, even in their minds, when looking at my body. I still tend to accommodate others who have strong feelings or preferences, so as not to 'rock the boat' to avoid dealing with fallout.

But over the years, I have learned that I *can* heal. I thank each and every person who has helped me on this journey toward wholeness. Because of these experiences, I have consistently fought for the underdog, shared my compassion for others who have been victimized, and worked tirelessly on issues of justice and fairness, with humility as well as a sense of courage against the odds. Fundamentally, our shared humanity is what heals us. Sharing this story continues my journey toward wholeness.

A BIGGER BODY

Anonymous

A list of things people have said to me about my weight, unsolicited:

"Why are you so fat?"
"You're not fat, you're just chubby, there's a difference."
"I always thought that if you just lost 20 pounds, you would be like, model beautiful."
"You have a goddess body."
"If I were fat, I would kill myself."
"Have you ever thought about ordering diet pills online?"
"It's so refreshing to have a teacher who doesn't have a typical yoga body."
"If you don't want to lose the weight for yourself, why don't you lose the weight for me, because I'm your partner and you love me?"
"Watch out for the big girl."

The last quote was from Lizzo. I needed Lizzo. We needed Lizzo. We, the big girls, the people in bigger bodies, the humans with bellies that America never put on the movie screen, or flaunted in every magazine. We needed her. Here she is. And here we are.

Most negative comments about my weight happened before I was 18. While it is true that children can be cruel, it's also true that they learn from the culture they are raised in. And in the early '90s to early '00s culture I grew up in, it was a fat-shaming free-for-all. It was the age of Fat Monica, Shallow Hal, The Nutty Professor, Bruce from Matilda, and Cartman. Whether it was from the media or from people's mouths, the message remained the same: to be fat is to be less worthy of respect.

I would be a millionaire if I had a penny for every time I heard a woman say, "Do I look fat?" to her friend in a public restroom while adjusting clothes in the mirror. How do you think that statement makes someone who actually lives in a bigger body feel? The message is clear: To be thin is to be better, more successful, worthy of love, more attractive. To be fat is to be worse, less worthy of love, less worthy of respect, and something to avoid being at all costs.

Many of the messages I hear and read on a daily basis are rooted in the belief that I am unworthy of existing simply for being in a bigger body. Even though I know this is inherently untrue, I am writing to release this lie from my consciousness. I want to tell you my story.

The last time I can remember being "skinny" was when I was around 6 years old. That may have been the first and only time, since I was born a whopping 10 pounds. A big, chunky, baby. It's cute to be chunky when you're a baby, though not as cute as a child or adult. Regardless of age, the reason may primarily be the same: genetics.

By the time I was 9 I had gained a lot of weight, as much of my family does at a certain age. It wasn't long before I learned that being bigger was cause for much heartache. From then on, the girls in elementary school stopped letting me sit with them at lunch, the boys picked me last in gym class, and the bullies who sat behind me routinely kicked my chair saying "Fat girl!"

The feelings of fear and isolation that came from these experiences slept inside me, under the surface, until I processed them later in many unhealthy ways. In college, I started heavily using alcohol and drugs. The next ten years of sedation led to depression, anxiety, and eventually suicidal thoughts. While the addiction to substances certainly fostered an environment for self-worthlessness, it is not what created it in the first place. I believe there is an even more worrisome connection between the messages I heard growing up fat, and my suicidal ideation later on. The message I internalized was: If I am worth less for being fat, am I worth anything at all?

My best friend from childhood and I have had strikingly similar experiences with body image insecurity, but only came to understand this in our late 20's. Recently, he dropped 85 pounds through the keto diet. It happened over the span of a year and a half, with frequent doctor visits to ensure his blood didn't become "mayonnaise," as he put it. There are pitfalls to the keto diet, but it had done what years of exercise, failed diets, and self-hatred had not: shed the weight. Instead of shedding his past with the weight, he became even more vocal in his advocacy for bigger-bodied people. That is because he noticed many bizarre changes in how other people treated him after he lost 85 pounds.

Before losing the weight, he was a struggling performer continually typecast as "the fat friend." Despite plenty of valuable experience and talent, the message he constantly received in auditions was: you are allowed to be funny, loud, and dumb. You are not allowed to be wise or dignified, and definitely never allowed to be a romantic lead. Yet how many times in real life does a person in a bigger body also happen to be smart, dignified, and in love? I'll tell you: all the time.

Once the weight was shed, he had access to all roles. In a thinner body, he could audition for whatever personality type he wanted. His characters were allowed to have varied interests, complex emotions, and were allowed to fall in love. Theatre directors weren't the only ones that treated him differently when he dropped the weight. Friends, family members, lovers, people in the grocery store, and really just about anyone he interacted with, approached him with more respect and patience. People were more willing to listen to him, to take him seriously, to ask him for advice. Though people were treating him differently, his experiences and his humanity had not changed much in a year and a half. He was still him, just thinner.

He noticed how people looked him in the eye more. Read that sentence again.

When he admitted this experience to me over coffee one afternoon, I was shocked. Not because I couldn't believe it, but because it was so relatable. Despite knowing each other for over twenty years, this was the first conversation in which we aired all of our shared grievances over body image and how the world treats fat people.

When discussing our self-destructive tendencies and how they may be related to negative body image, he said something that nearly made me jump out of my seat. He said that for years he subconsciously "liked to hide behind the weight." Now that the weight was gone, he couldn't hide behind it anymore. It made him wonder if somehow he had purposely kept the weight on as a sort of security blanket he could hide his vulnerability under.

Those words were gut-wrenching to me. For the first time, they lifted the veil over what I had been going through for a long time. That one sentence, "I liked to hide behind the weight," revealed so much about my own journey of self-healing.

Part of my inability to ever be truly skinny is attributed to genetics. My ancestry consists mainly of big-hipped, large-bellied, very tall and/or very round individuals. Genetics also played a role in my "pretty" features. Big green eyes, naturally straight blonde hair, clear skin, big boobs, and long legs are objectified by society just as much as one's weight.

As a child, my "prettiness" was already apparent, and I remember how people would look at me. They would say to my mother, "Oh she's so pretty!" I was like a doll, an object to be adored. I remember the way certain older men would stare at me. I remember it feeling wrong.

Approaching puberty, around age 9, I started to noticeably gain weight. This trend continued, with me dropping some weight in my tweens, then gaining again around age 15. I noticed that whenever I gained weight, people's behavior toward me changed. People would pass me by. They would look me in the eyes less often. They would not stop, point, stare, or mention my beauty to my parents. I kind of liked this. My fatness was my invisibility cloak.

I also noticed the male gaze on my body decrease. On a subconscious level, I knew that being a beautiful blonde girl with "appropriate dimensions" made me more of a target. So I perpetually and habitually put on weight to disappropriate my dimensions. To protect myself. To say, "No, this is not your body, it is mine. Look what I can do to it."

This part of my story is a fairly recent realization. It is difficult for me to fathom that I purposely kept weight on for years to de-sexualize myself, because it leads to another difficult realization—that sometimes gaining weight was my choice. It is difficult to come to terms with this because it sort of verifies what fat-shaming celebrities love to highlight: that weight gain or loss is within one's control. But in my case, that is still not entirely true.

Out of the answers that came from my friend's conversation, two concepts emerged that I am still exploring.

First, that while my thought process to gain weight in order to hide may have been validated by immediate experiences in my youth, I grew up to discover that fat people are sexualized just as much as anyone else. They're even fetishized. So is the real issue that our society promotes consent-less sexualization of people's bodies, rather than solely the obvious over-sexualization of skinny people?

The second is this: my subconscious need to keep weight on led to struggles with food addiction. Earlier I mentioned that I have struggled with addiction. Whenever I would give up one of my "big bad" addictions, I would uncover all the micro-addictions underneath. The shopping, the codependency, and the food. Food was what I could always fall back on when other substances weren't there. There are no age or legal limits on how much food you can keep in your car, your cabinet, or your body. The hole will never fill. When I'm in a state of obsessively eating, there is no sense of hunger or satiation. Similar to getting high, there is a sense of absolute need, devouring with no mindfulness, and then a feeling of regret afterward.

Many of the body-positive accounts I follow on social media discourage negative food talk. That is to say, thinking of eating as inherently bad. Or shaming people for "eating too much." But speaking from my own experience, admitting my issues with food addiction helps me to have a more positive relationship with food. This healthier relationship with food has not come out of a fat-phobic need to lose weight. It has come with lots of love and appreciation for my weight as it is. I walk 5 miles a day, I teach yoga, I am recovering from food addiction, and I am still, by society's standards, fat.

Even though losing or gaining weight may be within someone's control, subconsciously or consciously, you truly never know their story. I share these aspects of my story in the time of Lizzo, when many more people are coming forward with their stories—these stories of owning and celebrating bigger bodies along with all the talent, humor, and intellect housed within them.

I have so many other nourishing aspects of my life that have nothing to do with my weight. I have traveled the world, focused on education, and connected with my community through art. I have refused offers for diet pills and gym memberships simply because the focus of my life has never been to have a six-pack.

The realizations I've had about my weight are deeply personal. In no way do I speak for the diverse community of people around the world who live in bigger bodies. Anybody, in any body, has their own experiences, painful or joyful.

What's heaviest for me isn't the weight itself, but the weight the world puts on myself and others for simply being in a body. I only ask to be visible. To be worthy. To be looked in the eye.

IMMIGRANT

Nelly Bablumian

I never self-identified with the word "immigrant" until Donald.
Honestly! Instead I would say,
"I moved to this country when I was nine."
"My children will be first-generation Americans."
"I'm not from here."
"I'm a foreigner."

That was my word—foreigner. Sometimes alien, but only legally. I
considered immigrant to be closer to migrant, as in, 'those oppressed
and overworked migrant workers,' but the I-word for some reason
never applied to me.

And now that it has become a "bad" word in popular lexicon, or at least
a very loaded one, I've realized that of course I'm an immigrant. I've
just never really seen my story through a larger lens.

I've always focused on my personal trauma of being displaced, losing
everything I knew, and being put into school three days after arriving
without having any sort of conversation, support, or check-in from my
mom. I didn't even know any English! But that's my own beef with my
family (and to a large extent my culture) on how children are treated.
I've never really connected to another dislocated lost soul, or—ok, an
immigrant – about our experience. I've only told stories to American
friends and have seen a caricature reflected back at me.

When I first moved here, I remember everything being fantastical
about America—larger than life, paved in gold, possibilities flooding
in and dancing around, the giant stores that never ended, the lights, the
limitless options, the dream.

But the minute we arrived, it seemed that my parents' house was an
alien island surrounded by the culture I was quickly getting to know as
the most familiar. My parents held on to their customs fiercely. They
refused to compromise on how things were done and how children

were to act—particularly girls. I stayed out later and later and slept over at friends' houses, despite my parents' virulent protests and our constant battles. Their rules and expectations for me were abstract and ungrounded in anything I could see around me. Their way of life didn't fit into the new world they brought me into, and I didn't understand why I wasn't allowed to become part of it.

It wasn't my parents' fault that I never fit in, nor was it their fault that I felt and was treated like an alien when we went back to Armenia. I feel strange calling myself either Armenian or American (the hybrid 'Armenian-American' makes me cringe). I don't know what it means to have a home, though I try to find it in friends and activities like theatre and cooking. I feel a twinge of it sometimes before I pack up and move, yet again. And only for an hour or two, total, have I ever felt a true sense of belonging. In the end, I'm just an observer, an outsider, and now an immigrant, coming for the jobs of hard-working Americans.

Listen, I have my grandma on the other side, griping about how I'm not Armenian anymore, how I've become such a nasty "Americantzi"(American). I get it from both angles.

Here in the very core of my being, I yearn and yearn, and oh what I wouldn't do, what I wouldn't give (I don't have much), just to have a tribe. To belong, to be seen without expectations that I should do *this* because I'm *that*: a woman, or an Armenian, a young person, or someone in a relationship with a man.

Am I idealizing tribes? When you belong, do you really get treated like a human?
Who knows.

The more I travel, the more I shed the need to be anything like an accepted category. I'm coming to learn that the tribe I yearn for is the tribe I must forge for myself—in the family I create, the friendships I keep and build with love, and the community scattered around the world closest to my heart.

DRAGON SURPRISE

Anonymous

When I was in middle school, my parents enrolled me in a live drawing class at our local art studio. I was very passionate about fine art, especially drawing, and my parents encouraged me—to the point of allowing me to draw nude bodies far before I would see one by any other means.

I enjoyed the class, sketching alongside "real" artists and developing my skill. Studying bodies wasn't uncomfortable for me at all. I was fascinated by anatomy and loved tackling the difficult spots, like hands and feet. The only aspect that still made me nervous—with good reason—was the penis, which I would draw as a vague oval.

One day in class, our model was a young, fit man, probably in his late 20's or early 30's. Okay, I thought, this will be fine, despite that drawing a quasi-Olympian god is fairly boring compared to delicate wrinkles, folds of fat, and bunched up skin that I still find far more interesting. He disrobed, settled onto the model's platform, and arranged himself in a pose reminiscent of Jeff Goldblum's in *Jurassic Park*.

That's when I saw it. His dick… it was unlike anything I had ever seen. A tattoo of a red and purple dragon started on his lower pelvis and snaked down his crotch. Its neck wrapped around his penis, and the head ended at, well, the head. To top it all off, the tip of his dick was pierced with a thick silver ring.

I was floored. I didn't even know that a dick could be pierced. And why the dragon—was it supposed to be cool? Do women like that? Would I like that eventually? My little brain couldn't wrap itself around the pain aspect of it all.

We started to sketch, being very mature about it all. Then, at some point during the session, it happened. The dragon started to move. It shifted. It wiggled. Then it rose up and breathed its fire. A thick white substance leaked out of the dragon's mouth and landed on the model's chest.

No one moved. No one said a word. The model got up, put his robe back on, and suddenly class was over without any kind of acknowledgment of the insanely inappropriate event we had all just witnessed.

My parents picked me up and I went home, like any other week. Of course I didn't tell them—or anyone. Who would believe me? Regardless, I was not willing to risk my drawing class. No one from the studio talked to them either, which to this day I think is one of the craziest aspects of the whole event. Is this something that happens sometimes? Is this the price of art? These unspoken questions remain unanswered.

Since that baffling day, I have never seen another tattooed dick, never seen another dick piercing, and, most notably, never witnessed or even heard rumor of another man coming using only the powers of his mind.

FALSE STARTS

Greg Correll

I raised Molly because her mother—my teenage hippie sweetheart—
went mad.

Frequently institutionalized her last twenty years, she cut herself
endlessly, with razors and worse. A fixture at front range ERs, until
they refused to sew her up anymore. No viable skin left to sew, in some
places. Medicated herself with everything she could find. Her self-
destruction was epic, but so was her willpower. She waited so long to
end herself, waited until her beloved child was at least an adult.

A gifted, original painter and writer—though her journals became
incomprehensible—she loved our daughter every minute she was
herself. Modern medication would have saved her.

Molly, as an adult, forgave her.

The end.

I restarted my life story at 21 as a single father, muscling past breakdown
for her sake. Transformed myself into magic papa—had to, that's all—
and we grew up together, Molly and I.

Lived in France, where she started school. She had madcap experiences
as an actress and child model in Manhattan, while I started a design
career. When she was nine, I married Deborah and we had two more
brilliant, ferocious daughters. Life hummed, for a while.

In college, Molly fell apart, pulled herself together, then fell all the
way a decade later. Was kidnapped by a predator, rescued by Planned
Parenthood when he made her pregnant—but she recovered, big time.
Made a spectacular life for herself, built a career.

We were uplifted by her struggle and triumph.

The end.

In 2018, Molly died of a rare and vicious carcinoma. Hundreds of tumors in her lungs, pleural lining, heart, back, brain, liver, legs. A year of chemo and radiation, until Sloane Kettering decided that's that. Maxed out on pain drugs—kill-a-rhino level, constantly adjusted—but her severe allergy to morphine, inherited from me, made things problematic.

As in: screams, grunts, moans, and thrashing that got worse. Her last few months were indescribable.

As in: if I try to describe it now, I will die.

I carried her, sleeping, on the subway, for a million years, when she was small and it was just the two of us. Last year we sat with her in her dark apartment—me, Deb, her sisters—at-home hospice—because we promised her: all the way, no matter what. Held her hand and looked her in the eye as the light died.

The end.

I was diagnosed as retarded because I didn't talk until age 5. "Off in a world of my own," and got slapped regularly for it. I could read before kindergarten—my beloved Nana taught me—but the day I finally spoke—sang a hymn in the back seat, coming home from Sunday school—I got my first belting. For fooling him, with my silence.

I was no fool: If you talked, you got beat.

My siblings and I were cored by a rageaholic father with polio and a sentimental 1950s pill-popping mother who wanted to be an artist. Crying got beat out of us until pain didn't hurt, somewhere around 9. That's when he started training me to eat all my food, too, same way he trained my older brother Chris: Brussels sprouts jabbed down my throat with a fork, Mom squeezing my neck.

For several years, before and after I was 9—the Bad Years, we called them—they collaborated in a reign of terror, to make us *behave*, a charade for the public. At kissing distance we knew chaos and roundhouse rights, bare-ass beltings, again and again—why bare?—and worse: *waiting* for the belt.

We were rewarded for enduring it. Got buttered popcorn and fudge, *Walt Disney's Wonderful World of Color*, if we didn't cry, didn't fidget, could fake a happy face.

At 12 I came to life as a flower child—1967—after Mom divorced Dad. Well, after he had her committed for even *thinking* she could divorce him, and after thrice-weekly ECT, for five weeks. *Then* she divorced him.

After ten months of drug-addled truancy—and her gross neglect—I was sent back to Dad so Mom could have "freedom." Ran away, got caught, ran away again. Arrested in a drug raid at 14, kept as an incorrigible.

Here it comes.

In a St. Louis juvenile jail, I was raped, tortured, and humiliated for five days by three older boys. Guards permitted it. Happened to other boys, too, as young as 9. Later I had reconstructive surgery, a partial anusectomy. Suffered for years with fissures, which I left untreated because to remember some is to admit all—I never forgot, but *it was a long time ago*, and *I deserved it, right?* and *there's no going back.*

And later: *I have a child to raise.*

Narrowly avoided Boonville—look it up, I dare you—because Mom convinced the judge that she would handle me. Acted the part of a normal 9th grader. Worked for hippie crisis switchboards, peer counseling groups, and developed mad skills for getting over on people. Dissociated self-deception declared as total Gestalt honesty.

At 15 I slept with everyone, a precocious libertine pretending to be straight—*desperate* to be straight. Pretended I hadn't been in love with a boy at 11.

At 16 I quit school and moved into a commune, an emancipated minor.

Pretended I'd erased rapes, fixed fractured sexuality. *Boys don't tell.* Besides, nobody cares about rape in jail, even now.

The end.

When I was 17 I moved a lot, to avoid the draft and a reckoning. Wandered the Rockies on timberline trails, alone. Asleep for a day, awake for five, writing, drawing. Lost.

Even so, I got my GED and started university, three and a half years after rape. Walked off a nervous breakdown as a freshman—someone turned in something I wrote about castrating myself, but the school counselor told me it was *normal, stop worrying so much.* A year later, voilà! Molly's mom—a bisexual feminist—and I latched on, willfully blind to her madness, her secret self-cutting. We promptly had a child; soon after, she left me; soon after that, she handed me a bag of diapers and dollies, and said "I can't do this."

Those first weeks with Molly were an existential crisis. Wanted to run away again. Wanted to protect my sweet, precious baby. Wanted to die. Wanted to be a good man, to earn my beloved grandmother's respect. I resolved to be the Best Parent Ever.

Mostly, I did that very thing. Made a few terrible errors, but mostly, yeah, I did it.

The end.

For over 15 years, in hundreds of thousands of words, I've produced private, vivid evidence for my story. How I got normal. Got stuck, too, and then undone by the past. My daughters were grown, and needed me less—were surly, in ordinary teen ways—but if I wasn't magic papa then…what? No more nobility, no one to live for? I was sullen, bitter, just as my undamaged, unbeaten, successful children were finding their way. Over-reactions, withdrawals, grudges—it made no sense.

Well, of *course* it all came back, what was never really gone. No hidden memories, just compartmentalizing, rationalization. Memory was a blur from the side, then smack! into the middle of next week, then not-quite-enough-amnesia, after the blow. I wanted to forget, the way writers forget what came before the edit.

I had to re-learn crying as a middle-aged man. To prove I *could* cry, then to cry at last for old injuries, for what I would never have. I told Deb I was a crybaby when I was little, not stoic, the way she knew me to be. Seemed innocent enough. I felt compelled to skirt the edges, to avoid saying it. But I couldn't stop. Woke an endless dread that should have ended 48 years ago—when I was *rescued*, right?

Closure would not come. I squashed; memory came back. Then washout, one night, when all she could do was hold me while I told her, bits and pieces, the shrapnel in the wounds. Safe bits, isolated pieces— peeks, at the worst of it—but why? Why suddenly reveal fractures, and why the need, the terror, of saying? Afterward, to my ugliness in the bathroom mirror, I warned: *you came close you fucking idiot—don't goddamnit don't ever say—she'll leave you, the girls will hate you, fear you—no one will ever love you again—is that what you want?*

At first, she told me to let it go. *You are not your father.* Remember the good you did and do with your girls. I nodded *yes* and pretended to feel relief. Pretense might magically make me whole.

I will never be whole.

I perversely undid decades of numb self-protection. Impulsively cracked open those stoic defenses, talked to myself late at night, dared myself to *really* remember. During the day I got angry over gigantic nothings—*just like Dad*—and quashed that, or tried to. Hyper-vigilant control—but picking at unhealed scabs stained everything. After some hard luck with work and health, the whisper became a boom: *it will always go wrong. You deserve what you get—and it will be bad.*

Dad always comes home.

My lifelong inchoate insomnia grew fangs, became something else. A grinding, through long nights of despair. Permission to feel was permission to dread. *What is it?* my wife would ask, and I'd say plain, simple things that became ferocious and horrifying when they left my mouth—*why did I say that?*—wrenched out in long, unparsable sentences.

She was disgusted, frustrated, concerned. Pissed at my sullen withdrawals, tamped-down rages, grudges. What happened to the playful papa the girls wrestled with, who taught them, encouraged them? Who said *I love you* every day, knocked before entering, and was in all ways respectful and respectable? We began to understand: there's Something Wrong With Me. Worried I was truly crazy, though she never admitted that. To have said any of it was to have said it all.

I toiled for my children, my wife, the orphan, the widow, the slave, the outcast, the stranger. If I diminished their suffering, I earned the right to sleep. As daughters grew and the years rolled on, I could never do enough, so I increased my work week to 60 hours, 80 hours—night duty, on-call, more complex projects, bigger teams.

Fatherhood made me a better man? Yeah—but it was also a gigantic misdirection. We want it to be true, that generosity and lovingkindness triumph over brutality.

But permission to remember and feel made me disintegrate. I'm a long history of nobody home, an actor scrambling for his lines. I grin on cue, answer appropriately, and hide my trembling hands. Grief never dies, but we can be...what, whole again? *Such bullshit.* For some of us that's a cruel lie. For over five decades I've been deep undercover, playing roles.

Now that I'm awake enough to see, to understand what happened, I see this: one can only be whole when one *knows* whole, has had whole, as a child.

The work of the last few years—reinhabiting my entire life—was not some Road to Wellness. It was a frantic effort, a way of protecting myself while that feral boy in me, the truth-teller, clawed his way out. I was afraid he might undo decades of Do-Right Duty, make my legacy not diligent, daily effort but one sudden unforgivable rage, or a blow—just like Dad—and *even one time* means the curse lives on, the cycle never dies, Satan's on his throne. Or if I turn it inward, then what? Me, smashed on the concrete, head blown to smithereens, drowning in vomit.

Not the end.

I got help. Told someone—poor wife—then poor therapist—then poor children—but it made me strong enough to see how sick I was, and am still. I teeter into suicidal ideation almost daily, bang my head, tremor, and walk in circles, twist like a pretzel, and repeat words. Strong enough to be my authentic, massively fucked-up self, as it were.

I have no self-governance, so I control myself. Want to give up and leave so I have stamina. Determined to die clean, because I'm filth. Every woman is a daughter to me, her dignity my crusade, because I'm a lecherous satyr who would transgress in every way. Because of What Happened, I know what I am, what I must guard against.

I remember every cringe-worthy gaffe and error, every missed mark, unbidden. Every foolish lie and deliberate hurt. I see now that slapping, belting, and punching was only part of what Dad did to us — and how can I forgive being *anything* like him, even just critical, sullen? I put in the work for my children's sake, stopped the cycle of blows, but I did not eradicate him, or jail, or anything.

I am unforgivable, no matter what. *Why?*

Some grow up in the dark groves of relentless and hopeless, no-safe-day and watch-every-sign, fearing the quick angry hand. Have parents who never improved, never made amends. Parents who call you names as a joke, and never teach, never help with homework, never mention your future—except as a lost cause for *little idiots like you.*

I'm tired of trying to find an acceptable, accessible way to say it. Changing my life into a recognizable narrative—with oblique descriptions of violence, so as not to "fetishize," that modern grad school concept. Pre-digesting, for lucky ducks who had love and safety, had ordinary neurotics for parents. I'm tired of uplift, closure, and other artful pretties.

Tired of pretending to be other than what I am: an existential thing, no longer afraid of the pavement below, who stays here only because I promised my children they would not *get the call.* I am an old, stiff, tremoring man who would tear those guards to bloody pieces.

I dream of self-immolation on the steps of the Missouri Department of Corrections.

I dream of forgiving them, all of them, every trudging soul.

All else is pretense and dishonest—because my ferocity is true, my ecstatic wonder is real, and I *was* waylaid. I am haunted and beautiful, just like this old world.

If you would know what it is, what it feels like, what was stolen, what survives—as a bird tracks in the sky, here and gone, observed and let go—I open like a flower for you. So would you, if you were me.

Hard to be detested and never know why; then beloved and never feel it. The best I saw as a boy came to me with my eyes closed. There was no rescue. But my eyes are open now, and I see it all.

I WANT YOU HEALTHY:
MUSINGS ON MY BODY AND SPIRIT
POSSESSED BY LYME AND OTHER DEMONS

Nelly Bablumian

I keep hearing the well-intentioned voices of my tribespeople chanting, "I want you healthy!" and it makes me want to shut my door and be alone with my pain. I need to keep this relationship sacred, don't need to run away from its wisdom.

I want to cradle myself in the womb of darkness, where my illness is subtly breaking my spine, infesting my body, and fulfilling my deepest fears. Let me keep my curtains drawn!

It seems we got it all wrong. It is not a failure to be sick. Do you hear me?

Do you believe me? Sometimes I don't, either. Sometimes, when I try to inhabit the lofty mindset of creating my own reality, I wonder what I did to make my body so broken—where I went wrong. But down here on earth, we mortals feel pain without having done anything to deserve it.

I am not wrong. I am just sick.

And here is the chant I keep coming back to that allows me to breathe:

It is OK to be sick.

It is OK to be sick. I believe sickness is the body telling us to listen deeper, to change course, to let go—to stay home. Sickness is a natural reaction to our lives, and to the insane world in which we live. We humans rush through our lives, our minds fluttered with anxiety, our spirits undernourished and disconnected, insatiably devouring our accomplishments and tossing them into a bottomless pit of daily to-do lists while thoughtlessly poisoning our environment and ourselves— and then we feel we've done something personally wrong when we're not well.

We falter in our ability to face our pain, wanting desperately to get better, to be healthy, to find a solution that will "fix it," and fast, too.

But what will I miss if I hurry through my pain?

When I got diagnosed with Lyme, everyone I knew was bursting with well-intentioned solutions. Drastic diets, herbal protocols, acupuncture, antibiotics, probiotics, bone broths, past life regressions, a trip to Germany or India, or a stay in a secluded cabin on the plains (that one was my favorite). I felt it was all coming from this frantic need to solve the problem, to find a solution—to fix it.

Don't get me wrong, I've tried most of these suggestions. Just these past few weeks, I've had sessions in massage, acupuncture, kinesiology, raindrop therapy, floatation therapy, crystal therapy, chiropractic, and guided meditation, and have taken tinctures and supplements, too. On and on I go, groping around in the dark for the thing that will WORK.

Wanting to get better is not a crazy reaction to being sick, nor is wanting others to get better. We are human, after all. Yet when I grasp for solutions, I'm acting from my urge to run away from the conversation, from all the discomfort I feel sitting with myself in silence, facing my inevitable demise.

I imagine that seeing a loved one sick reminds a person of how desperately they're holding on to their own fragile health. How terrifying is it that a tiny little tick, albeit vile and bloodthirsty, could leave a person bedridden, unable to work or remember their appointments or even why they walked into a room, longing for months to take a single pain-free breath? It's scary to think that it's not something that will go away in a week like a cold, or something stressed-induced that can be meditated back into balance.

Being well is such a vague and elusive concept. We want to keep getting better all the time, to keep striving for the perfect body, the perfect state of mind, forgetting that every day we're getting closer and closer to the moment when something will kill us. And that will not be a failure, either. That is the way of all living beings. It is.

Eckhart Tolle has this to say about it:

"The ego says, 'I shouldn't have to suffer,' and that thought makes you suffer so much more. It is a distortion of the truth, which is always paradoxical. The truth is that you need to say 'yes' to suffering before you can transcend it."

Let's not add despair on top of our suffering. Instead of the mantra, "I want you healthy," let's take a breath and say, "I'll meet you where you are."

MY "DEAR FRIEND"

Harriet

Once upon a time, in a small village in Upstate New York... no... no... wait a minute. This is not a fairy tale or a pathway to Mother Goose and her rhymes, nor a visitation to the texts of the Brothers Grimm. It's a dark and stark memory that has lived inside of me for almost 18 years. A true story I have carried in my head and heart all of this time. A story that is tainted and stained with guilt—my guilt. It goes with me wherever I go. It is a constant companion. Perhaps this is an opportunity to release it, or at least diminish its impact on me. Perhaps I will be exonerated. I don't know what's possible, I won't know until I complete this task, if I am able to. This is not my first attempt. It's the fourth.

Please bear with me.
How many times?
How many times did he do it?
How many times did he unbutton his pants, unzip his fly, pull out his shirt and pull down his underwear? How could he do it? What did he do? I want to know. It's years later and I still want to know.

All these questions I neglected to ask him as he stood before me that morning. Our living room was transformed into a confessional, and I was the priestess on hand. I am the one who sat there before the clock struck seven as he walked into the house with that look. The look of repentance.

"Is there something you want to tell me?" I asked as I sat there in my pajamas and bathrobe. Not priestess attire at all. But I knew. I knew it for months. I sensed it. I could feel it. My body shivers at the thought of it. I always knew. He and his wife were our dear friends. Very dear friends. How could he? He was the one who emerged from the shadow world and walked the earth. He entered the room, closed the door, undid the button to his pants, unzipped the zipper. Yes, he was a man whose dark side prevailed, and sexual gratification, titillation, stimulation was his quest. My mother, my 94-year-old mother, was his golden fleece, the holy grail, the treasure from King Tut's tomb, the 1848 gold rush. "How many times?" No, once was not enough to satisfy him, was it? He sat on the floor in front of me. "How many times?" I was still counting up the possible number of times as he whispered to me, "I don't remember." Just once could not have satiated his appetite, which he fed behind our own closed doors... and I knew.

Shame on me. Me, who worked with survivors of sexual abuse and incest. Me, who should have known. Me, who should have trusted my instinct. Me, who always told people to trust their feelings and intuition, because there is something there. Me!

On Wednesday nights, my husband had a weekly sauna. Afterward, the sauna bums (a term of endearment on my part), would come up to the house and have a meal, sit, engage in conversation and/or turn on the telly. After a while, our friend, our 'dear friend' would stand up, excuse himself and say, "I'm going to look in on Gertrude." I told my husband I wasn't comfortable with the situation. "You're being paranoid," he replied. He wouldn't dare entertain my fears. Why? Why didn't I look in on her? Why didn't I ensure her safety and well-being? Why didn't I protect her? That was one of the main reasons I never considered a home for her. She would always be safe with us. Always.

Me, who denied my own mother, Gertrude, the safety of a home to dream in and live in with a peaceful state of mind. My innocent mother with Alzheimer's paid with her spirit, while I live(d) with the horror of it all.

My mother, small, wrapped within the safety of her bed, embarking on a wonderful sleep and entering her dreamworld. Was she awake when he stood over her? He was so tall, a silhouette of the night. What did she think? What did she see? What did she feel? Gertrude, the perfect prey. Would she remember? Who would have believed her if she had pointed her index finger in his direction and said "J'accuse"?

There was this wonderful, loving, compassionate person, Mariyanna, whom I hired to help out when I couldn't be home. That day, that infamous day of shame and discovery, I had to run an errand. Mariyanna stayed with my mother, but had to leave before I returned. On her way home, she realized she left her purse in my mother's room. She turned around, made her way into my mother's space, and opened the door to her bedroom. There he stood, tucking in his shirt, zipping up his zipper, buttoning his pants. He looked at her and ran out. I pulled up, got out of my vehicle, and carried my grocery bags into the house. Mariyanna came out of my mother's room.

"Mariyanna," I embraced her. "What's wrong?"
"You know your 'dear friend?' "

She proceeded to tell me what transpired. I ran into my mother's room. She was crying, a deep but silent cry, then it turned woeful as she grabbed my hand and pulled me down to her side. I brushed her cheek. I held her close. Her heart beat like a kettle drum, and mine played in harmony with hers. My tears joined her tears, and Mariyanna's joined ours, as we embarked on a journey of grief, rage, and betrayal. Yes, our 'dear friend', our "I'm-going-to-look-in-on-Gertrude" friend would pay for these heinous crimes he committed. I brushed her hair from her face, placed my hands on her cheeks, and wiped away her tears. As I looked at her, I knew I was the one who should have had Gertrude's index finger pointed in my direction—I was the guilty party. "J'accuse!"

That night, after the sauna, I told my husband what transpired.
"No! No way. You're being paranoid again."
When I told him what Mariyanna witnessed, he went quiet.
"I'm going to call the police," I said. "I'm going to report him."
"No, Harriett, you can't. He has children. What about his wife? She's one of your best friends."
"Yeah... and so was he. I'm going to tell her. She needs to know."

"How many times...?" I asked again. He begged forgiveness. Head bent down, he sat in front of me and shared his life story. Yes, it was a tragic story, and I had some compassion for him. I named one of his daughters when she was born. We were all close. But forgiveness... forgiveness for coming into our home and sexually molesting my mother as we sat in our living room? And then coming back to be one of the boys again, laughing and joking after getting his jollies off with my mother. My mother Gertrude. Gertrude with Alzheimer's. And if she cried out, I don't know, where was I? Did she call for help? Did she say no? Did she say stop?

"What were you thinking? What did you see when you looked at this helpless innocent 94-year-old woman? My mother. How could you do it? Tell me. I want to know. Have you ever done this before, with someone else?"

He looked up at me and went quiet.

My husband implored me not to call the police. But I wanted people to know what this "dear friend" of ours was capable of. How would I do it? His wife was my best friend. His children were a part of our lives. And my mother—what about her?

I asked him to leave. Later that morning, I called his wife. I shared the story of her husband's actions in great detail. I waited to hear something emanate from her lips: a response, a sound, an inhalation or an exhalation—something. But there was nothing. What was she thinking? Feeling? What did he say to her? I told her that he needed counseling, and gave her the name and phone number of a therapist.

I never saw him again. I often wondered if I would see him, perhaps walking along a road while driving my van....could I do it?

My mother Gertrude left this world as we know it on October 28th, 2005.

Every morning when I wash my face, brush my teeth, braid my hair, I look into the mirror and see myself looking back. When I see my reflection in a window or my shadow created by the sun shining behind me as I walk the roads and pathways of the world I live in, I remember. Inside my head I hear, "Why didn't I...?"

J'accuse...

NEVERENDING STORIES HAVE ENDINGS

Elizabeth Gross

This is my anecdotal version of a tale that has been told by women for lifetimes on end.

—

I was a wide-eyed 19-year-old women's studies major who found myself invited into the quaint homes of DIY punk grlz. We ate vegan cast iron skillet meals made from a mixture of dumpster-dived and freshly picked farm veggies, which poured over their kitchen tables alongside mason jars embraced by crocheted cozies.

I met him within that world. There he was one cool summer afternoon, standing on their lawn, a captivating smile on his face as he sipped a lime seltzer. I was taken aback by how unusually beautiful he was. My eyes zeroed in on his heart-shaped lips, and I pondered the possibility of them one day touching mine.

While I felt all these pleasures upon first meeting him, my intuition entered the scene, urging me to maintain distance. I became aware of subtle things that felt confusing to me, like how his smile seemed to push me away while it simultaneously drew me in. I resolved to let this fascinating dilemma of mutual attraction and caution unfold on its own.

Throughout those first years of knowing him, I responded to his offerings of guidance and friendship in ways that honored my intuition's request for distance, yet also felt quite warm and tender. As I watched him move through relationships with women over those years, I felt both jealous of and sorry for them. The homes they created together were filled with charm, yet also strangely foreboding. My attention wandered past the enchanting books and herbal potions lining their walls to the atmospheres within, which always seemed distinctly cold and thick.

Every now and then I asked myself what it would be like to be in a relationship with him, and always came back to reservation. Yet, one night in my early 20s, I boldly told him that I knew one day we would "have our time." The look he gave me in that moonlit moment was one I came to know well later on: one of fused pain and longing. The sad desperation in his eyes told of the love he wanted so badly and hadn't found quite yet.

Flash forward to age 30. I had just moved into a beautiful cottage, committed to focusing wholly on my healing there. I also felt ready for deep romantic love. At that time, he and I were part of a group that explored concepts related to consent. After one of our meetings, he hung back to talk. My attraction to him was as strong then as it was the first time I met him. While the caution was still there, I chose to favor the attraction. I asked him if he remembered that moment years prior, when I foresaw us being together. He did. I said that feeling hadn't changed for me. He admitted the feeling was mutual. Our confession bled into one of the most alchemical embraces I've ever experienced. It felt like stardust.

The beginning of our relationship was absolutely magical. Our conversations were rich and validating, lasting for hours on end. Our lovemaking felt safe and healing. We wrapped around each other and kissed under starry skies. He asked if he could call our relationship "The Neverending Story," the name of my favorite childhood tale. It felt like a dream come true.

Yet within our honeymoon swirl, I felt my boundaries dissipate. His lifetime research of the paranormal took a conversational driver's seat, even though I didn't share his interest in the topic. I convinced myself that I needed to become accustomed to these concepts, which seemed so fundamental to his being. Yet the evil nature of that world, as he portrayed it, frightened me. I felt a portal open up through which existential dread began to pour. My once hopeful perspective became riddled with chaos. I felt haunted at night, as if dark beings hovered over me while I tried to sleep. Whenever he slept alongside me, those dark forces seemed to disappear. He confirmed that he felt as if he spent those nights warding off demons. He became my knight in shining armor in the strangest way, giving me moments of relief from my now anxious reality.

One weekend, a simultaneous eclipse and blizzard welcomed cabin fever to settle in. At some point while settling in for the night, I casually mentioned that I had reached out to his ex, who had just taught a class I went to and loved. At that moment, the seemingly perfect cocoon we had formed together morphed into a horrible tempest.

"YOU REACHED OUT TO HER?! WHO WOULD DO THAT!?" He roared. He writhed. I was utterly shocked. Just as he couldn't understand what I had done, I couldn't understand how he was reacting. His stress response was charged with a profound anger over which he seemed to have no self-regulation, and it scared me.

That night, as I drifted off disturbed alongside his eerily tranquil slumber, a friend and former lover entered my dreams. This lover appeared outside my cottage, pounding on its fog-covered windows, calling to me over and over: *"Pay attention to your dreams!"* As I blankly stared at him from inside, a heavy hand grabbed my shoulder. I spun around to see my new lover there. He appeared as a monstrous version of himself, with grey skin, black eyes, a long beak and razor-sharp teeth. He became bigger and bigger as I became smaller and smaller. Miniature me watched in horror, entirely frozen, as eventually he took up the whole height of my cottage. I woke up in a panic, horrified by what the dream could mean about what was to come.

I felt myself spinning into a twilight zone, where my wonderful dream world began to turn into a nightmare. It seemed a silent deed was written by which I became indebted to him for reaching out to his ex, and the penalty for this wrongdoing was wholly tending to his needs while erasing my own. As I signed the invisible contract, I resolved to do enough good to atone for my crime and bring us back into balance. I chose to frame what we were going through as a challenge. If I persevered, our relationship would transform into the epic love I knew it could be.

I focused on his heart-shaped lips, the ones I had dreamed of kissing years before, and prayed that they would cease spitting hate and embrace me with love. Yet he only dove more deeply into relentless criticism about the world around him, seemingly ignited by my interaction with his ex. It felt as if a ghost he had created in her name entered our relationship, and was haunting our every step. I figured his disdain for her was personal, but his many other judgments of women began to surface.

He began detailing things women did that "didn't work for him," such as wearing makeup and form-fitting clothing, shaving, and posting body-exposing pictures on social media. He ranted about how women acquiesced to the perverted male gaze by hugging men upon hellos and wearing leggings as pants. It all seemed like one huge "she was asking for it" conversation, yet he was so convincing that I began to doubt my own credibility as a feminist. I stopped wearing makeup and shaving, switched out form-fitting clothes for baggy ones, and ceased social media sharing. I faintly recalled the 19-year-old feminist I had been when we first met, wondering where she had gone and why he didn't accept who she had become.

The elephant in the room called misogyny continued to set up shop, taking the form of judgments about my general interactions with men. A standard greeting hug with a man launched him into an unyielding shame rant. His rage led me to shut off exchanges with other men almost entirely, even those I considered to be dear friends.

Ridicule of my interactions with men bled into ridicule of my past sexual experiences. What I had vulnerably shared at the beginning of the relationship became fuel for his now incessantly disparaging remarks. He preached that the energy of my past partners lingered inside my body, and he questioned whether or not he could be with me because of it. His distorted perceptions, not my actual truth, became reason for him to regard me as an unworthy partner. My sexual past became so inflated and cockeyed from his point of view that I also came to regard it as flawed, even the parts that were actually quite healthy.

Our own sexual exchanges shifted from nourishing acts to something quite different. When I told him I didn't want to have intercourse while menstruating, it triggered his rage. My uterus felt wounded, as if physically punched by his invalidation, yet I didn't feel safe enough to communicate my hurt. After that incident, he lashed out angrily if anything disrupted his orgasm, as if I were entirely responsible for its fulfillment. He urged me to quiet down, calm down, and practice restraint for my desires. My pleasure not mattering became part of the protocol.

In order to secure emotional safety, I began withholding information from him. I deleted texts with loved ones asking for guidance about what I was going through. I hid feminist books friends gifted me after he saw their titles and expressed bold offense. The story of how I was sexually assaulted while traveling abroad years prior felt like it could be used to mark another check on my slut list, so I withheld it. When he found out that his ex came regularly to my yoga class, he demanded I tell him every time she came, so he could know more about her than she seemed to want him to. I stopped teaching my yoga class instead. I became the crone in folktales who rushes the princess off in order to save her from the beast.

Devaluation became so woven into our relationship that I didn't know who I was anymore. He scorned me for laughing at things I thought were funny, so I stopped laughing. He scorned me for stretching my body after a long day of sitting, so I stopped stretching. He told me I was too intense and emotional, so I stopped expressing how I felt. All of a sudden I was a child again, being told I was an "idiot who doesn't know what she's talking about," like my father had said so many times before.

As the months progressed, our relationship worsened. I couldn't do anything right by him. I tried with all of my might to win back his love and acceptance, unaware that those outcomes were beyond my control. I became so preoccupied with saving the relationship that I didn't prepare for my upcoming move, which needed to happen as my rental lease was coming to an end. I didn't have enough energy to discern what would be the healthiest option for me, so I chose the most readily available solution of moving in with my parents, who had recently bought a home nearby. If I had been in a clearer headspace, I never would have chosen that option, but at the time I was too deflated to strategize in my favor. I felt broken inside.

Both of us moved in the same month, into two separate homes. After giving my all and showing up for him with countless boxes moved and hours of time spent, he broke up with me. The breakup process felt entirely rushed, as if he just wanted it over and done with. I felt absolutely used, as if he endured the relationship just long enough to reap the benefits of my precious cottage life. Throughout that time, he took herbal baths I prepared for him, ate my home-cooked meals, made love with me in my big cozy bed, and nurtured his rage in the privacy of my secluded home. When the time came that I could no longer provide those things to him, he discarded me.

Shortly after our breakup, he casually asked if I had ever heard of "The Neverending Story." At that moment, I realized that our neverending story had truly come to an end.

Not too long thereafter, I had quite a telling dream. In this dream I was in nature, surrounded by naked and beautiful bodies free of shame. As I realized it was safe for me to be entirely myself alongside them, I saw him in the distance, convulsing on the ground. I ran to him as fast as I could, grabbing a doctor by the hand along the way. We arrived to find him dying. I urged the doctor to help, but the doctor seemed unconcerned. The doctor looked straight into his eyes and asked him plainly: "What do you feel?" He abruptly ceased convulsing and shifted into a terrifyingly hollow state. He gazed back at the doctor and replied, "Nothing." The doctor looked at me with a loving smile and took my hand. We walked off together, back into the crowd of life.

With the guidance of countless walks in nature, amazing friends who provided unconditionally loving support, and commitment to a self-focused recovery process, I was able to take the equally relieving and painful steps of saying goodbye to him. Establishing strong boundaries went against many of my patterns and pangs, yet I knew I had to focus entirely on cultivating a loving and trusting relationship with myself. I'm learning that what I was yearning to feel from him are feelings I can conjure from within. Letting go of him has helped me redirect my focus on what it means to take care of myself, a commitment which I believe will only strengthen as my healing unfolds.

My ancestry contains a line of women who endured partnerships with emotionally abusive men. These matriarchs, bound to men who didn't know how to manage their own life traumas, endured horror in silence in order to maintain security within the family dynamic. But the thing about secrets is, they always find a way to be told. I know the tales my grandmothers kept silent because they live in my bones. What am I supposed to do with this knowledge, with these unsung songs of grief? Continue to endure relationships with charming men sporting blue beards? No matter how familiar that pattern feels to my cells, I have to stop its momentum. The healing has to begin with me.

"I hope you will go out and let stories, that is life, happen to you, and that you will work with these stories...
water them with your blood and tears and laughter till they bloom, till you yourself burst into bloom.
That is the work.
The only work."

— CLARISSA PINKOLA ESTÉS

OUR DEEPEST THANKS

All our GoFundMe donors who helped this book
become what you now hold in your hands.
We especially want to thank:
Alexandra Alberto
Daryl and Suzanne Anderson
Krista Kaufman

Our GoFundMe gift contributors:
Chris Cunningham and Loupe Print
Fine Artist Noëlle Cunningham
Sasha Geerken and Sasha Botanica
Rachel Firak and Fawn and Flora Soaps
Filmmaker Dylan Reid

Jeuneé Godsey and Jenny Moore for your editorial assistance
Greg Correll for your publishing assistance

To our authors and to you, our reader,
without whom this book would not be possible.